Business Correspondence

Letters,
Faxes,
and
Memos

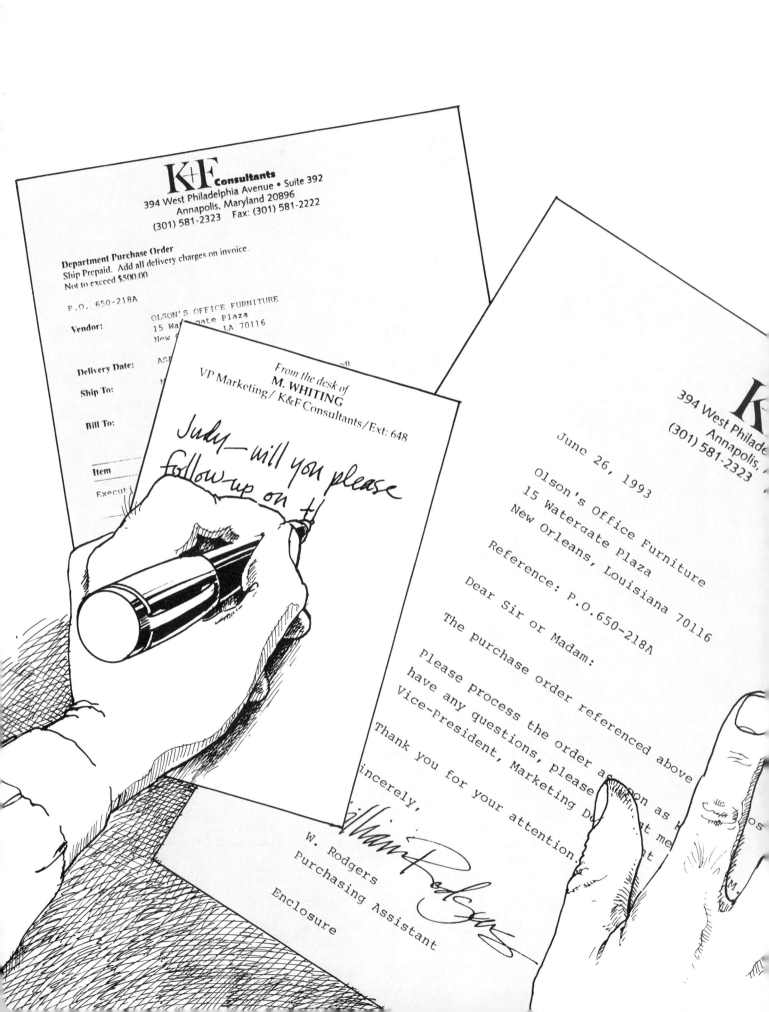

K+F Consultants
394 West Philadelphia Avenue • Suite 392
Annapolis, Maryland 20896
(301) 581-2323   Fax: (301) 581-2222

Department Purchase Order
Ship Prepaid. Add all delivery charges on invoice.
Not to exceed $500.00

P.O. 650-218A

Vendor: OLSON'S OFFICE FURNITURE
           15 Watergate Plaza
           New O_____   LA 70116

Delivery Date: AS_____

Ship To:

Bill To:

Item

Execut_

From the desk of
M. WHITING
VP Marketing/ K&F Consultants/Ext: 648

Judy— will you please
*follow-up on t_*

---

394 West Philade_
Annapolis,
(301) 581-2323

June 26, 1993

Olson's Office Furniture
15 Watergate Plaza
New Orleans, Louisiana 70116

Reference: P.O.650-218A

Dear Sir or Madam:

The purchase order referenced above

Please process the order as soon as

have any questions, please

Vice-President, Marketing D_

Thank you for your attention.

Sincerely,

W. Rodgers
Purchasing Assistant

Enclosure

BUSINESS CORRESPONDENCE

**Letters,
Faxes,
and
Memos**

Lin Lougheed

Addison-Wesley Publishing Company, Inc.

Reading, Massachusetts • Menlo Park, California • New York
Don Mills, Ontario • Wokingham, England • Amsterdam
Bonn • Sydney • Singapore • Tokyo • Madrid • San Juan
Paris • Seoul • Milan • Mexico City • Taipei

Product Development Director
Judith M. Bittinger

Editorial
Elinor Chamas, Karen Doyle

Manufacturing/Production
James W. Gibbons

Text Design
Graphic Associates

Cover Design
Will Winslow

Illustrations
Will Winslow

The author would like to acknowledge and thank the teachers and students
whose comments and advice refined the text. The author is especially
appreciative of the insightful suggestions of Bonita Vander, Vice President,
Education, SCS Business and Technical Institute.

SCS Business and Technical Institutes, New York and Philadelphia
Geraldine Jacob, Y. Kokosinski, Robert Nester, Jeanne J. Newman,
Edward Pack, Giovanna Rick, John Sitter

Wilson Adult School, Arlington, VA
Suzanne Grant, Susan Huss, Betty Lynch, Inaam Mansoor, Sharon McKay,
Donna Moss, Kenwyn Schaffner

Willston Center, Falls Church, VA
Shujaat Ali, Peggy Seufert Bosco, Eva Dadok, Carolyn McCarthy, Son Nam Nguyen

IDI Editorial Staff and Production Assistants
Anne Kennedy, Gina Richardson, Donna Barth, Charles Buck, Helen Papp

Contents

MODEL SECTION

REFERENCE SECTION

A Letter To You

Addison-Wesley Publishing Company
1 JACOB WAY
READING, MASSACHUSETTS 01867

(617) 944-3700

May 18, 1992

Dear Reader:

I wrote Business Correspondence for you. It will help you become a successful member of an office "team." You will learn how to write clear and effective letters, faxes, and memos. You will learn common expressions and procedures used in business. You will also improve your basic English skills.

This book is divided into two sections: Models and References. The Model Section provides examples of the most common types of correspondence, with grammar exercises and lots of practice in preparing letters, faxes, and memos. The Reference Section is a summary of all you have learned in the Model Section. Use it to look up information quickly. For even more extra practice, there are additional exercises in each part of the Reference Section.

You may use this book with or without a teacher. All the answers are in the Answer Key at the end of the Reference Section. In some Practice Letters, numbers at the left are used in the Answer Key to help you find the answers. You can correct your own work and build your business skills. Good Luck!

Sincerely yours,

Lin Lougheed

Lin Lougheed

Test Yourself

▶ **A. Label the parts of this letter.**
  B. What is the format of this letter: block, semi-block, or indented?
  C. Correct the underlined errors.

The answers are on Page 138. If you need help, study the Reference Section. After you finish this book, try the test again. You will see a big improvement!

Polycomp International
459–34 Grand Hotel Avenue
Taipei, Taiwan

1 august 15 1994

2 mr. Gilbert m Ramirez

3 Vice President, Marketing

4 soup and Salads Restaurants

5 5632 Western Avenue

6 Los angeles, California 90026

7 Mr dear ramirez

8 your letter of March 15 arrived this morning

9 Tell us your travel plans and we'll meet you at the airport?

10 We appreciate your interest in our compan-

11 y and look forward to your visit next month.

12 Sincerly yours

13 *Bill Chang*

14 bill Chang

15 President

1A

Applying for a Job

WORDS TO KNOW

advertisement (ad)
(to) apply
applicants
appreciate
(to) confirm
employment
(to) enclose
enclosure
Human Resources Director
interest
job
office manager
position
receptionist
resumé
(to) schedule
secretary
stationery
wpm (words per minute)

▶**Read this conversation.**

Annette: I need a job, Pat.

Pat: What kind of a job, Annette?

Annette: I want to be a secretary.

Pat: Look at this ad in the newspaper.

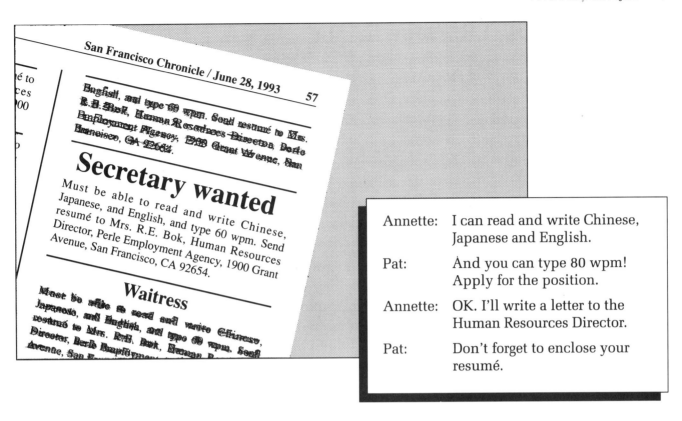

San Francisco Chronicle / June 28, 1993   57

English, and type 60 wpm. Send resumé to Mrs.
R.E. Bok, Human Resources Director, Perle
Employment Agency, 1900 Grant Avenue, San
Francisco, CA 92654.

Secretary wanted

Must be able to read and write Chinese,
Japanese, and English, and type 60 wpm. Send
resumé to Mrs. R.E. Bok, Human Resources
Director, Perle Employment Agency, 1900 Grant
Avenue, San Francisco, CA 92654.

Waitress

Must be able to read and write Chinese,
Japanese, and English, and type 60 wpm. Send
resumé to Mrs. R.E. Bok, Human R...
Director, Perle Employmen...
Avenue, San F...

Annette:	I can read and write Chinese, Japanese and English.
Pat:	And you can type 80 wpm! Apply for the position.
Annette:	OK. I'll write a letter to the Human Resources Director.
Pat:	Don't forget to enclose your resumé.

▶ *Complete each sentence with a word from the box.*

Example:

Annette is applying for the _____*position*_____ of secretary.

1. Annette will write a letter to the _____ .

2. Perle Employment Agency needs a _____ .

3. Annette needs a _____ .

4. She will _____ for the position of secretary.

5. Annette saw the _____ in the *San Francisco Chronicle.*

advertisement (ad)
(to) apply
Human Resources Director
job
position
secretary

COMMON BUSINESS EXPRESSIONS

In many companies the title of the person who hires new employees is *Human Resources Director.* In other companies the title of this person is *Personnel Director.*

MODEL LETTER: Applying for a Job

▶ *Annette Lee is applying for the job.*
Read her letter.

▶ *Circle the correct answer.*

1. Who wrote the letter?
   A. Mrs. Bok
   B. Annette Lee

2. Who is the letter to?
   A. Mrs. Bok
   B. Annette Lee

3. Where does Annette live?
   A. 1900 Grant Avenue
   B. 16 North Road

4. What did Annette enclose?
   A. The San Francisco Chronicle
   B. Her resumé

5. What is Mrs. Bok's title?
   A. Human Resources Director
   B. Secretary

6. When was the letter written?
   A. June 28
   B. June 29

```
                          16 North Road
                          Berkeley, California 95436
                          June 29, 1993

Mrs. R. E. Bok
Human Resources Director
Perle Employment Agency
1900 Grant Avenue
San Francisco, California 92654

Dear Mrs. Bok:

        I am applying for the position of
secretary which was advertised in the San
Francisco Chronicle of June 28.

        I have enclosed my resumé, and I
would like to schedule an interview. I will
call you early next week.

        I look forward to discussing this
position with you.

                    Sincerely yours,

                    Annette Lee
                    Annette Lee


Enclosure
```

GOOD BUSINESS NOTE

"Follow-up" is very important. After you send the letter, you should call the employer. In your letter give either general or specific times to call.

General: I will call you early next week.

Specific: I will call you Monday or Tuesday.

This keeps your name in front of an employer.

BUSINESS STYLE: Body of an Application Letter

A letter of application generally has four parts.

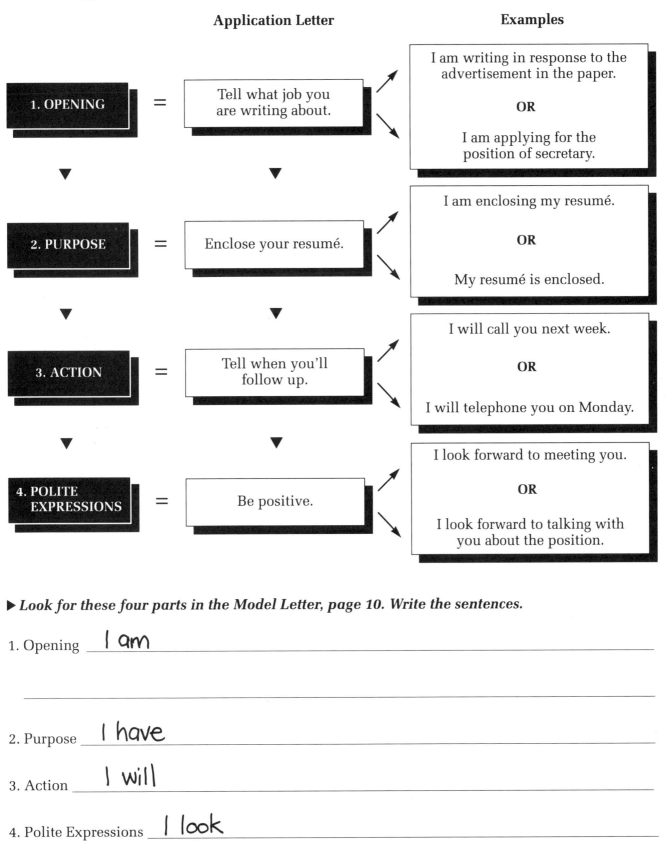

Application Letter   **Examples**

1. OPENING = Tell what job you are writing about.

I am writing in response to the advertisement in the paper.

OR

I am applying for the position of secretary.

2. PURPOSE = Enclose your resumé.

I am enclosing my resumé.

OR

My resumé is enclosed.

3. ACTION = Tell when you'll follow up.

I will call you next week.

OR

I will telephone you on Monday.

4. POLITE EXPRESSIONS = Be positive.

I look forward to meeting you.

OR

I look forward to talking with you about the position.

▶ *Look for these four parts in the Model Letter, page 10. Write the sentences.*

1. Opening   I am _____

_____

2. Purpose   I have _____

3. Action   I will _____

4. Polite Expressions   I look _____

PUNCTUATION: Greetings

Colon

Use a colon (:) after the greeting in a formal, business letter.

  Dear Mrs. Bok:

  Dear Sirs:

  Dear Madam:

Comma

Use a comma (,) after the greeting in an informal, personal letter.

  Dear Mother,

  Dear Richard,

Period

These titles end in periods.

Mr. Smith	Any man
Ms. Schwinn	Any woman
Dr. Ross	A man or woman who is a medical doctor (M.D.) or who has an academic degree (Ph.D.)
Mrs. Jones	A married or widowed woman

▶ *Write the greeting. Use the correct punctuation.*

Example:

Mr A P Safeway _____ *Dear Mr. Safeway* _____

1. Mr James A Smith (your friend) _____

2. Mrs Ann Smith _____

3. John R Marker MD _____

4. Mr Ralph Tenley _____

5. Ms Susan Grant (your cousin) _____

6. Ms Augusta Lee _____

7. Mrs Martha Walpole (your sister) _____

GRAMMAR: Subject/Verb Agreement

The subject and verb must agree in number. If the subject is singular, the verb must be singular.

Example:

Singular Subject	**Singular Verb**	
The letter	is	on the desk.
The secretary	types	the letter.

If the subject is plural, the verb must be plural.

Example:

Plural Subject	**Plural Verb**	
The letters	are	on the desk.
The secretaries	type	the letters.

	Third person Singular			**Plural**
He	writes	They		write
She	wants			want
It	was			were
	has			have
	is			are

▶ *Complete the sentences.*

was   *were*

1. The secretaries _____ on time yesterday.

2. The Human Resources Director _____ in her office all last week.

want   *wants*

3. Mary _____ to apply for the position.

4. Fred and Henry _____ new jobs.

writes   *write*

5. Jim _____ well.

6. We often _____ letters to each other.

has   *have*

7. He _____ enclosed his resumé.

8. They _____ enclosed their resumés.

are   *is*

9. There _____ only one job.

10. There _____ many applicants for the job.

BUSINESS STYLE: Formal or Informal

Use formal English in business letters.

Informal English	Formal English
I want...	I would like...
I want a new position.	I would like a new position.
I want to be a secretary.	I would like to be a secretary.

GOOD BUSINESS NOTE

Be very careful when you type business letters. Errors do not make a good impression.

▶ *Change these sentences to formal English.*

Example:

I want to schedule an interview.

I would like to schedule an interview.

1. I want a new job.

   _____

2. I want an interview.

   _____

3. I want to apply for the position.

   _____

4. I want to enclose my resumé.

   _____

5. I want to call you soon.

   _____

6. I want to change jobs.

   _____

Letter Practice 1

▶ *Dorothy Jones answered this ad from the Milwaukee Post. Correct the 10 errors in her letter. Write your answers on the list.*

Milwaukee Post
August 16, 1994

Secretary wanted. Must have experience. Send resumé to Mr. Frederick Wolf, Director of Marketing, Smith Printing Company, 590 Sixth Avenue, Milwaukee, Wisconsin 53216.

~~Must be able to read and write Chinese, Japanese, and English, and type 60 wpm. Send resumé to Mrs. ... Post ...~~

```
                    5695 South 23rd Road
                    Milwaukee; (1) Wisconsin 53217
                    August 16, 1994

Mr. Frederick Wolf
Director of Marketing
Smith Printing Company
Sixth Avenue 590 (2)
Milwaukee, Wisconsin 53216

Dear Mr. Wolf,. (3)
     I is (4) applying for the positin (5)
of secratary (6) which were (7) advertised
in the Milwaukee Post of August 16.
     I has (8) enclosed my resumé; and I
want (9) to schedule an interview. I will
call you early next week.

     I look forward to discussing this
position with you.

                    Sincerly (10) yours,

                    Dorothy Jones
                    Dorothy Jones

Enclosure
```

Type of Error	Correction
1. Punctuation	_____
2. Word order	_____
3. Punctuation	_____
4. Grammar	_____
5. Spelling	_____
6. Spelling	_____
7. Grammar	_____
8. Grammar	_____
9. Style	_____
10. Spelling	_____

COMMON BUSINESS EXPRESSIONS

Positive expressions end most letters. When you write, use positive expressions like these.

I look forward to
- meeting you.
- talking with you.
- working with you.

Letter Practice 2

▶ *Complete the sentences in this letter. Use the advertisement and the appropriate words from the box.*

Publisher's Monthly
July 16, 1993

File Clerk wanted. Must have high school education. Send resumé to Mr. Paul Rook, Human Resources Director, Rascott Printing, 200 East 57th Street, New York, NY 10010.

am	July	Monthly	my	Street	yours
East	like	Mr.	position	week	

_____

_____ (Write your

_____ address here)

July 17, 1993

_____ Paul Rook

Human Resources Director

Rascott Printing

200 _____ 57th _____

New York, New York 10018

Dear _____ Rook:

    I _____ applying for the _____ of

file clerk which was advertised in the _____ 16

Publisher's _____ .

    I have enclosed _____ resumé, and I would

_____ to schedule an interview. I will call you

early next _____ .

    I look forward to discussing this position with you.

        Sincerely _____ ,
        (Write your name here)

        (Print your name here)

Enclosure

Test Yourself

HONG KONG TIMES
AUGUST 9, 1994

Receptionist wanted. Must speak Chinese and English. Send resumé to Ms. Jane Goodman, World Communications, 64 Delrosa Avenue, Los Angeles, CA 90027.

~~Must be able to read and write Chinese, Japanese, and English, and type 60 wpm. Send~~

▶ *Answer these questions.*

1. Where was this position advertised?

   Hong Kong _____

2. What was the date of the ad?

   August_____ , 1994

3. What is the position?

   _____

4. Where do you write?

   Ms. Jane _____

   World _____

   64 Delrosa _____

   Los Angeles, _____ 90027

▶ *Write a letter of application below.*

MODEL LETTER: Replying to an Applicant

▶ *Circle the correct answer.*

1. Is the letter from Mrs. Bok?

   A. Yes   B. No

2. Is the letter on company stationery?

   A. Yes   B. No

3. Did Mrs. Bok receive Annette's resumé?

   A. Yes   B. No

4. Did Annette already get the job?

   A. Yes   B. No

5. Did Perle Employment fill the position?

   A. Yes   B. No

6. Will Annette have an interview on Monday?

   A. Yes   B. No

PERLE EMPLOYMENT AGENCY

1900 Grant Avenue
San Francisco, CA 92654
415-625-1110
FAX 415-424-5251

July 3, 1993

Ms. Annette Lee
16 North Road
Berkeley, California 95204

Dear Ms. Lee:

Thank you for sending your letter and resumé.

We appreciate your interest in the Perle Employment Agency. We would like to schedule an interview on Monday, July 8 at 9 a.m. Please call us to confirm the time.

We look forward to talking with you.

Sincerely yours,

Mrs. R. E. Bok
Human Resources Director

COMMON BUSINESS EXPRESSIONS

Letterhead and Logo
The return address on a business letter is usually printed on the stationery. The pre-printed return address is called a letterhead. The artwork or graphic design is called the logo. When there is a letterhead, the secretary does not need to type the return address — only the date.

ZIP Codes and Postal Codes
The post offices in most countries use letter and/or numbers to sort mail. In the United States, these numbers are called ZIP Codes. In other countries they are called postal codes.

BUSINESS STYLE: Body of a Reply to an Applicant Letter

A reply to an application letter generally has four parts.

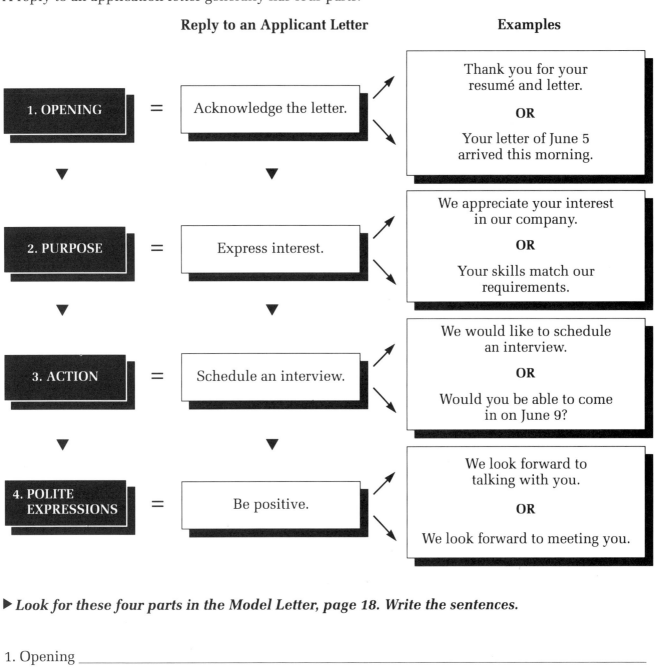

Reply to an Applicant Letter	Examples

▶ *Look for these four parts in the Model Letter, page 18. Write the sentences.*

1. Opening _____

2. Purpose _____

3. Action _____

4. Polite Expressions _____

GRAMMAR: Capitalization

These words are capitalized:

A. The first word of a sentence

B. Proper nouns: names, cities, states

C. Titles when they are written before a name

D. The names of organizations and companies

E. The days of the week, months of the year, and holidays

F. The first word in the greeting

G. The first word of the closing

▶ *Capitalize the following words. Write the letter of the rule above that gives the reason.*

Example:		**Rule**
mr. Smith	*Mr. Smith*	C

1. july _____ ____

2. dear Mary _____ ____

3. international systems co _____ ____

4. there are many applicants _____ ____

5. chicago _____ ____

6. sincerely _____ ____

7. thanksgiving _____ ____

8. monday _____ ____

9. dr Winslow _____ ____

10. los angeles, California _____ ____

▶ *Correct the capitalization errors. Write the capital letter over the error. There are 22 errors.*

Gift Galleries
105 West Lake Drive
Sydney, New South Wales
2007, Australia
252-787-6600
FAX 252-786-5600

1 february 28, 1992

2 mr. andrew pan
3 63 fifth street
4 melbourne, 2085 victoria
5 australia

6 dear mr. pan:

7 thank you for sending your letter and resumé. they
8 arrived on february 22.

9 we appreciate your interest in gift galleries, and
10 we would like to schedule an interview on wednesday,
11 March 6 at 9:00 a.m. please call to confirm.

12 we look forward to meeting you.

13 sincerely yours,

14 *Bill Reston*

15 Bill Reston
16 Human Resources Director

17 Enclosure

GRAMMAR: Prepositions

at + (hour)

We will see you *at 9:00 a.m.*

Let's have lunch *at noon.*

on + (day of the week)

We will see you *on Friday.*

My appointment is *on Monday.*

on + (month + day)

Your resumé arrived *on June 7.*

I called *on January 26.*

of + (month + day)

I received your letter *of May 15.*

The ad was in the Boston Times *of June 3rd.*

▶ *Complete the sentences with the prepositions* **at, on** *or* **of.**

1. Your letter _____ June 16 was received on June 20.

2. My appointment with the Human Resources Director is _____ 5:00 p.m.

3. The interview is _____ Friday.

4. The post office closes _____ 12:30.

5. The letter was mailed _____ November 7.

6. The ad was in the *Publisher's Monthly* _____ January 19.

Letter Practice 1

▶ *Correct the errors. Write the answers above the errors.*

Type of Error	Number of Errors
Capitalization	10
Prepositions	3

NEWSBOOK, INC.
The Newsbook Building
Livingston, New Jersey 07039
201-5911-2113
FAX 201-592-7782

1 September 10, 1993

2 Mikinori Hiratsuma

3 4390 Nagata

4 tokyo, 100 japan

5 dear mr. hiratsuma:

6 Thank you for sending your letter and resumé. They arrived

7 in september 8.

8 we appreciate your interest in <u>Newsbook</u>, and we would like

9 to schedule an interview at tuesday, September 13 on 10:30

10 a.m. please call us to confirm.

11 We look forward to talking with you.

12 sincerely yours,

13 *Jean Ryan*

14 Jean Ryan

15 Human Resources Director

16 BR/st

Letter Practice 2

▶ *Complete the sentences with an appropriate word or phrase from the box.*

letter	on	resumé
like	on	Shop-A-Lot
Mr.	Reilly	yours

Shop-A-Lot Inc.
100 Washington Street
Scranton, Pennsylvania 18504
717-992-8000
FAX 717-992-8181

February 17, 1993

Mr. William Reilly
96 Columbia Road
Austin, Texas 78746

Dear_____:

Thank you for sending your _____ and _____. They

arrived _____ February 15.

We appreciate your interest in _____-____-____, and we would

_____ to schedule an interview _____ Wednesday,

February 25 at 2:30 p.m. Please call us to confirm.

We look forward to talking with you.

Sincerely _____,

Stanley Price

Stanley Price

Human Resources Director

SP/jk

Test Yourself

▶ *You are Mr. Price's secretary. Follow his instructions.*

From the desk of
Stanley Price

Write a letter to Kimberly Thompson. Her address is 46 Equator Avenue, New Haven, Connecticut 06520. Schedule an interview on Monday, February 23 at 1:00.

Shop-A-Lot Inc.
100 Washington Street
Scranton, Pennsylvania 18504

2A

Requesting a Service

WORDS TO KNOW

(to) attend

attendance

audiovisual

conference

(to) confirm

(to) contact

deadline

(to) discuss

equipment

facilities

(to) meet

meeting

plan

planner

planning

(to) reserve

reservation

sales meeting

(to) serve

▶ *Curt talks to Ms. Jan Turner, a Meeting Planner at Arrowhead Conference Center.*

Jan :   Yes, Mr. Marks, we'd be glad to help you plan your meeting. When is your meeting?

Curt: March 15th to the 17th.

Jan: How many people will attend?

Curt: About 50...or maybe 80. I'll get back to you on that.

Jan: Please do. I'll send you a checklist to help you plan everything. Fill out the checklist and then we'll confirm the plans.

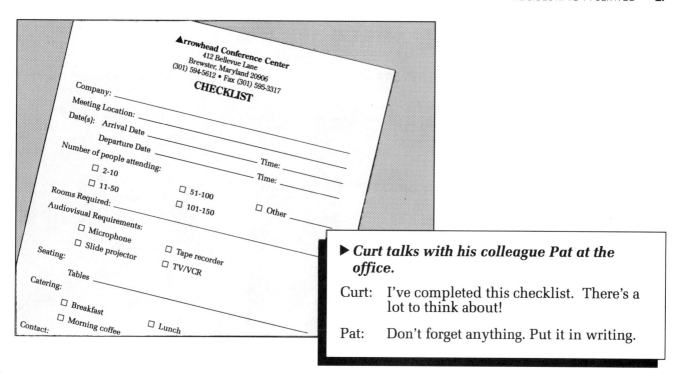

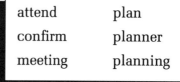

▶ **Curt talks with his colleague Pat at the office.**

Curt: I've completed this checklist. There's a lot to think about!

Pat: Don't forget anything. Put it in writing.

▶ *Complete each sentence with a word from the box.*

attend	plan
confirm	planner
meeting	planning

Example:

Mr. Marks has to ___plan___ a meeting.

1. Ms. Turner is a meeting _____ . She helps people plan meetings.

2. How many people will _____ the meeting?

3. Fifty to eighty people will attend the _____ .

4. Ms. Turner will do the _____ .

5. Ms. Turner will _____ the plans.

COMMON BUSINESS EXPRESSIONS

Get back to someone = Write or call someone again with more information.

Put it in writing. = Write down what you say.

MODEL LETTER: Requesting a Service

▶ *Mr. Curt Marks writes a letter to Ms. Jan Turner to confirm his request. Read the letter.*

● ● ● CELLULAR PHONE COMPANY
● ● ● 10 Harbor Place
● ● ● Baltimore, Maryland 21220
● ● ● 301-792-5522
FAX 301-792-5557

January 17, 1993

Jan Turner
Arrowhead Conference Center
412 Bellevue Lane
Brewster, Maryland 20906

Dear Ms. Turner:

In our telephone conversation yesterday, we discussed plans for our meeting at your conference center. I would like to confirm these plans.

The meeting will be from March 15th to the 17th. We will need two rooms. Eighty people will attend the meeting.

I have additional requests:

• Could you provide ten tables for each room?
• Is it possible to have a TV and VCR in one room?
• Would you be able to serve lunch on the 16th?

I would appreciate your answers by next Friday. If you need any more information, please call me.

I would like to thank you for your help in planning our meeting.

Sincerely yours,

Curt Marks

Curt Marks
Special Projects Office

CM/ls

▶ *Circle the correct answer.*

1. Who wrote the letter?
   A. Curt Marks
   B. Jan Turner

2. Who received the letter?
   A. Curt Marks
   B. Jan Turner

3. Where does Curt work?
   A. Brewster, MD
   B. Baltimore, MD

4. What audiovisual equipment do they need?
   A. A microphone
   B. A TV and VCR

5. How many additional requests are there?
   A. Three
   B. Four

GOOD BUSINESS NOTE
Always write a letter to confirm information after an important conversation. This avoids misunderstandings.

BUSINESS STYLE: Body of a Letter Requesting a Service

A letter requesting a service generally has four parts.

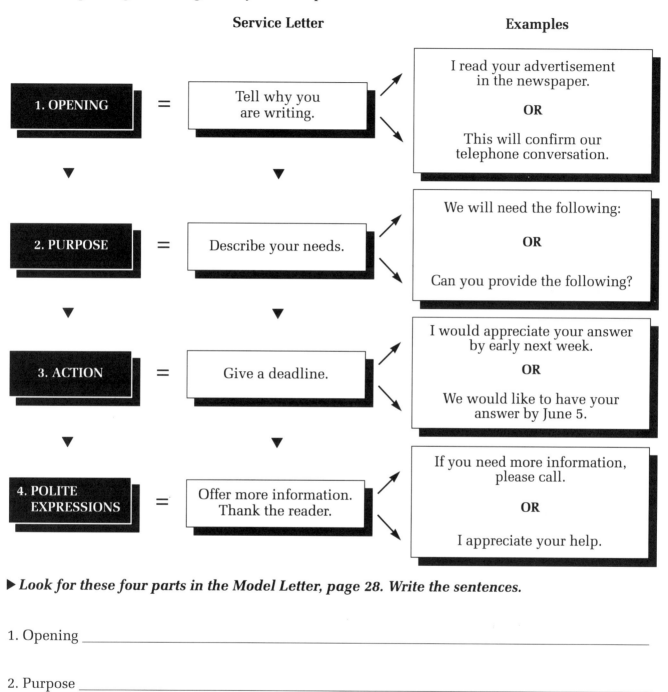

Service Letter | Examples

1. OPENING = Tell why you are writing.

I read your advertisement in the newspaper.

OR

This will confirm our telephone conversation.

2. PURPOSE = Describe your needs.

We will need the following:

OR

Can you provide the following?

3. ACTION = Give a deadline.

I would appreciate your answer by early next week.

OR

We would like to have your answer by June 5.

4. POLITE EXPRESSIONS = Offer more information. Thank the reader.

If you need more information, please call.

OR

I appreciate your help.

▶ *Look for these four parts in the Model Letter, page 28. Write the sentences.*

1. Opening _____

2. Purpose _____

3. Action _____

4a. Polite Expressions _____

4b. Polite Expressions _____

GRAMMAR: Question Types

There are two question forms in written English:
Yes/No questions begin with an auxiliary word.

Auxiliary	Subject	Verb.....?	Answer
Do	you	know the answer?	Yes, I do.
Is	the meeting	confirmed for Friday?	No, it isn't.
Will	you	serve lunch?	Yes, we will.
Could	you	provide ten tables?	Yes, I could.

▶ *Circle the correct answer*

Example:

May we take a coffee break?

(A.) Yes, you may.   B. No, you don't.

1. Do you need help?

    A. No, you won't.   B. No, I don't.

2. Did you eat lunch yet?

    A. Yes, I did.   B. Yes, I do.

3. Has the secretary arrived?

    A. Yes, she did.   B. No, she hasn't.

4. Will they come early?

    A. No, they aren't.   B. Yes, they will.

5. Has the equipment been ordered?

    A. Yes, it has.   B. Yes, they have.

6. Did you attend the class?

    A. Yes, I will.   B. Yes, I did.

7. Could you plan the meeting?

    A. No, I couldn't.   B. No, I won't.

8. Will he meet his deadline?

    A. Yes, he will.   B. Yes, he could.

GOOD BUSINESS NOTE

Deadlines are a part of business. When you give your suppliers a deadline, you help them serve you better.

You must type this by tomorrow at 10:00.
Your deadline is tomorrow at 10:00.

Wh- Questions begin with a question word.

Question Word	Auxiliary + Subject ?	Answer
When	is the meeting?	On October 13th.
Who	is the meeting planner	Jan Turner.
Where	will the meeting be	In the conference room

▶ *Complete the questions with words from the box.*

How long	Who	What
How many	Where	When

Example:

Who is Jan Turner?
She is a meeting planner.

1. _____ furniture is needed?
Tables and chairs.

2. _____ will the meeting last?
For three days, from Monday to Wednesday.

3. _____ does the meeting begin?
It begins on Monday, March 15 at 8:30 a.m.

4. _____ will the meeting be held?
At the Arrowhead Conference Center.

5. _____ will attend?
Thirty people will attend.

▶ *Circle the correct answer.*

1. Is the meeting on March 25?
   A. At the hotel.   B. No, it isn't.

2. When did the meeting start?
   A. An hour ago.   B. Yes, it has.

3. May we take a break?
   A. Fifteen minutes.   B. Yes, you may.

4. Will coffee be served?
   A. About 10:00 a.m.   B. Yes, it will.

5. What do you need?
   A. A VCR.   B. No, I don't.

6. Do you want to attend?
   A. Yes, I do.   B. At 6:00 p.m.

PUNCTUATION: Questions and Sentences

Question Mark

Use a question mark (?) at the end of a question.

> Do you have any questions?

> What equipment will you need?

▶ *Put a question mark (?) or a period (.) where necessary.*

Period

Use a period (.) at the end of a sentence.

> If you have any questions, please call.

> We will need a VCR.

Type of Error	Number of Errors
Question mark	6
Period	3

INTERNATIONAL CONFERENCE CENTER
50 Rockefeller Plaza
New York, NY 10019
212-574-1256 ● FAX 212-576-6621

1 August 17, 1993

2 Makiko Sato
3 Project Coordinator
4 BMC Engineering Corporation
5 50 Webster Center
6 New Haven, Connecticut 06500

7 Dear Ms. Sato:

8 Thank you for your telephone call this morning

9 International Conference Center is pleased to plan
10 your next meeting   Could you please answer the
11 following questions

12 How many rooms will you require
13 How many people will attend your meeting
14 What are the dates of the meeting
15 What audiovisual equipment will you require
16 Which meals would you like catered

17 I look forward to hearing from you

18 Sincerely yours,
19 *Joseph Pace*
20 Joseph Pace
21 Meeting Planner

22 JP/rs

BUSINESS STYLE: Using a Checklist

▶ *Arrowhead Conference Center has a checklist to help plan meetings. Use the information in the Model Letter on page 28 to fill in the checklist.*

▲rrowhead Conference Center
412 Bellevue Lane
Brewster, Maryland 20906
(301) 594-5612 • Fax (301) 595-3317

CHECKLIST

Company: _____

Meeting Location: _____

Date(s): Arrival Date _____ Time: _____

Departure Date _____ Time: _____

Number of people attending:

☐ 2-10   ☐ 51-100   ☐ Other _____

☐ 11-50   ☐ 101-150

Rooms Required: _____

Audiovisual Requirements:

☐ Microphone   ☐ Tape recorder

☐ Slide projector ☐ TV/VCR

Seating:

Tables _____

Catering:

☐ Breakfast   ☐ Lunch   ☐ Reception

☐ Morning coffee   ☐ Afternoon coffee ☐ Dinner

Contact:

Name: _____

Department: _____

Telephone: _____ Fax: _____

Letter Practice 1

▶ *Correct the errors.*

Type of Error	Number of Errors
Word order	2
Punctuation	5
Capitalization	4
Spelling	1
Formal vs. Informal	1

WRT RADIO
1 Longman Plaza
White Plains, New York 10504
914-793-8156 FAX 914-793-8885

1 April 13, 1994

2 Joseph Pace
3 International Conference Center
4 50 Rockefeller Plaza
5 New York, new york 10019

6 Dear Pace Mr.

7 in our telephone conversation of April 12, 1994, we discussed
8 plans for our meeting at your conference center. I want to
9 confirm these plans.

10 The meeting will be from september 15 to 17, 1994?   We will
11 need 5 rooms. Approximately 50 people will attend the
12 meeting. We will need microphones in each room, We will
13 only serve coffee at the breaks coffee.

14 We have additional requests:

15   It is possible to have a TV and VCR in each room?
16   Would you be able to serve lunch on the 16th

17 Could you please respond to these requests by April 20, 1991.
18 If you need any more information, please call me.

19 I appreciate your help in planning our meeting.

20 Sincerly yours,

21 *[signature: Mary Smith]*

22 Mary Smith
23 Special Projects

24 MS/gl

Letter Practice 2

▶ *Use the checklist and words from the box to complete the sentences.*

Checklist
Company: *Argyle Sock Company*
Meeting location: *Int'l Conf. Center*
Date: *March 15-19, 1994*
Number of people attending: *150*
Number of rooms: *5*
Audiovisual equipment: *Microphones*
Catering: *Coffee breaks*

Argyle Sock Company 48 Foxhall Crescent
Missoula, Montana 59037
406-998-1458
FAX 406-994-0125

September 17, 1993

Joseph Pace
International Conference Center
50 Rockefeller Plaza
New York, New York 10019

attend	conversation	plans
breaks	March	questions
confirm	microphone	rooms

Dear Mr. Pace:

In our telephone _____ of September 15, 1993,
we discussed _____ for our meeting at your
conference center.   I would like to _____ these plans.

The meeting will be from _____ 15-19, 1994.   We will need
5 _____ Approximately 150 people will _____
the meeting.

We have additional requests:

Is it possible to have a _____ in each room?
Would you be able to serve coffee at the coffee_____ ?

Could you please respond by early next week?   Do not hesitate to call me if
you have any _____ .

I appreciate your assistance in planning this meeting.

Sincerely yours,

Ron Allerton
Assistant to the President

RA/fg

Test Yourself

▶ *Write a letter on page 37 from Brian Ross to Mr. Joseph Pace at the International Conference Center. Look at the checklist for the information.*

▲rrowhead Conference Center
412 Bellevue Lane
Brewster, Maryland 20906
(301) 594-5612 • Fax (301) 595-3317

CHECKLIST

Company: _Basic Shoe Company_

Meeting Location: _International Conference Center_

Date(s):   Arrival Date _Nov. 5_   Time: _9:00_

Departure Date _Nov. 8_   Time: _5:00_

Number of people attending:

☐ 2-10   ☐ 51-100   ☑ Other _200_

☐ 11-50   ☐ 101-150

Rooms Required: _2_

Audiovisual Requirements:

☑ Microphone   ☐ Tape recorder

☐ Slide projector   ☐ TV/VCR

Seating:

Tables _____

Catering:

☐ Breakfast   ☑ Lunch   ☐ Reception

☐ Morning coffee   ☐ Afternoon coffee   ☐ Dinner

Contact:

Name: _Brian Ross_

Department: _Marketing Department_

Telephone: _(703) 662-0736_   Fax: _(703) 662-0739_

B A S I C
Shoe Company
621 Wilson Boulevard
Arlington, Virginia 22207
(703) 662-0736

MODEL LETTER: Confirming a Service

▶ *Read the letter.*

▲rrowhead Conference Center
412 Bellevue Lane
Brewster, Maryland 20906
(301) 594-5612 • Fax (301) 595-3317

January 22, 1993

Curt Marks
Special Projects Office
CELLULAR PHONE COMPANY
10 Harbor Place
Baltimore, Maryland 21220

Dear Mr. Marks:

Thank you for your January 17 letter expressing interest in the Arrowhead Conference Center. This letter will confirm our plans for your meeting.

We understand that your company would like to reserve two rooms from March 15 to March 17. Approximately eighty people will attend your meeting.

As you requested, we will provide twenty tables—ten in each room. We will also have a television and a VCR available in one room. We will serve lunch on the 16th.

If you have any questions or need to make any changes, please contact me immediately.

We look forward to seeing you on March 15.

Sincerely yours,

Jan Turner

Mrs. Jan Turner
Meeting Planner

cc:M. Dubois, Audiovisual Department

JT/kk

▶ *Circle the correct answer.*

1. Who is planning a meeting for Mr. Marks?
   A. Mrs. Dubois   B. Mrs. Turner

2. When was Mrs. Turner's letter written?
   A. January 17   B. January 22

3. Why was this letter written?
   A. To reserve five rooms.
   B. To confirm information.

4. Can Mr. Marks make changes?
   A. Yes   B. No

5. Where will the conference take place?
   A. In Baltimore   B. In Brewster

6. Who received a copy of this letter?
   A. M. Dubois   B. J. Turner

BUSINESS STYLE: Body of a Letter Confirming Plans

A confirmation letter generally has three parts. The *Action* section is not necessary.

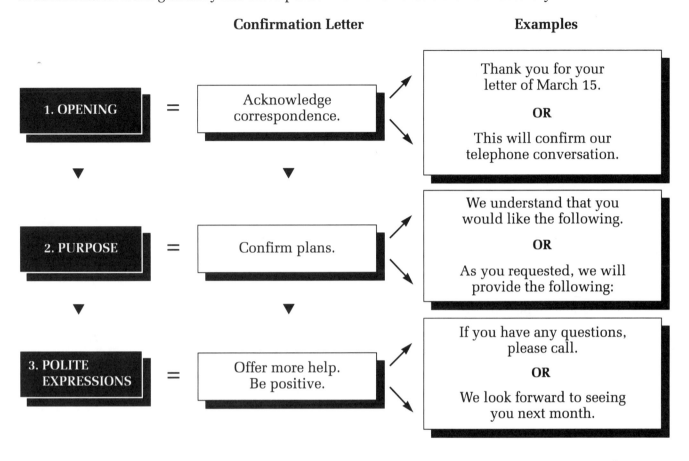

Confirmation Letter	Examples

▶ *Look for these three parts in the Model Letter, page 38. Write the sentences.*

1. Opening _____

2. Purpose _____

3a. Polite Expressions _____

3b. Polite Expressions _____

GRAMMAR: Pronouns
A pronoun refers to something or someone already mentioned (the referent).

Subject Pronouns		Object Pronouns	
I	we	me	us
you	you	you	you
he	they	him	them
she		her	
it		it	

Example:

Mr. Jones is the manager. He has worked here for fifteen years.

Who is the manager? _Mr. Jones_   What is the pronoun? _He_

Who is Mr. Jones? _The manager_   What is the referent? _Mr. Jones_

Who is "he?" _Mr. Jones_

▶ *Answer the following questions.*

1. The managers planned their meeting.
   They will meet on April 2.

   What is the pronoun? _____

   What is the referent? _____

2. The receptionist sat at his desk.
   He answered the phone.

   What is the pronoun? _____

   What is the referent? _____

3. The Vice President read her memo.
   She called her secretary.

   What is the pronoun? _____

   What is the referent? _____

4. The planner closed his books.
   He opened his file cabinet.

   What is the pronoun? _____

   What is the referent? _____

▶ *Circle all the pronouns and their referents. Put a 1 next to the sentence that should come first. The referent should always come first.*

Example:

____   The technician came to fix (it.)

_1_   (The VCR) is broken.

1. ____   The secretary will read it after lunch.

   ____   The mail just arrived.

2. ____   The manager is on the phone.

   ____   He's talking to a client.

3. ____   They need to be put away.

   ____   The files are on top of the cabinet.

4. ____   They expect 100 people to attend.

   ____   The sales personnel are having a meeting.

▶ *Complete these sentences with the correct object pronoun. The pronoun referent is underlined.*

Example:
We need <u>these memos</u> typed today.

Can you type __*them*__ before 5:00 p.m.?

1. <u>I</u> received the letter.

   The letter was sent to _____.

2. We received your <u>confirmation</u>.

   We put _____ in your file.

3. <u>She</u> took the telephone message.

   Ask _____ what the number was.

4. The meeting <u>planners</u> did not arrive until 10:00 a.m.

   We wanted _____ to come earlier.

5. <u>We</u> cancelled the conference.

   The hotel could not give _____ enough rooms.

Possessive Adjectives		Possessive Pronouns	
my	our	mine	ours
your	your	yours	yours
her	their	hers	theirs
his		his	
its		its	

▶ *Complete the sentences.*

Example:

Her   Hers

__*Her*__ letters are missing.

Mine   My

1. _____ company's name is Argyle Socks.

your   yours

2. This equipment is _____.

Their   Theirs

3. _____ sales meeting will be at the Hilton.

We   Our

4. _____ lunch will be served shortly.

ours   our

5. These conference rooms are _____.

Letter Practice 1

▶ *Read Ms. Paganos' notes.*

Checklist
Company: *Norton Publishing Company*
Meeting Location: *Pacific Conference Center*

Date: *6/20 -21*
Number of people attending: *100*
A-V equipment: *microphone, slide projector*

Seating: *about 20 tables*
Catering: *Morning coffee and lunch*
Contact: *Jill Martin (TEL# 413-331-0768)*

▶ *Correct the errors.*

Type of Error	Number of Errors
Capitalization	10
Punctuation	4
Grammar	2
Spelling	1
Word order	2

Pacific Conference Center
918 West Park Avenue • San Francisco,CA 91237
415-591-0013 • FAX 415-591-1300

1 January 13, 1995

2 Jill martin Ms.
3 Norton Publishing Company
4 1500 Adams Stret
5 Quincy ma 02176

6 Ms. Martin dear:

7 Thank your for your June 12 telephone call expressing
8 interest in the Pacific Conference Center This letter will
9 confirm our plans for your meeting.

10 we understand that your compny would like to reserve two
11 rooms at our facilities from June 20 to June 21.
12 Approximately 100 people will attend your meeting.

13 As you requested, we will provide twenty tables—ten in each
14 room. All of the rooms have a microphone and a slide
15 projector. Us will serve morning coffee and lunch on both days.

16 if you have any questions or need to make any changes, please
17 contact me immediately?

18 We looks forward to seeing you on June 20.

19 sincerely,

20 *Katherine Paganos*

21 katherine Paganos
22 Project Manager

23 cc:f jones
24 kp/jk

Letter Practice 2

▶ *Complete the sentences with words from the box.*

our	we
your	me
you	

Englewood Golf Club
54 ROUTE 9
ENGLEWOOD CLIFFS, NEW JERSEY 07632
203-787-2135 • FAX 203-788-2236

April 20, 1994

Martin Green
5765 Lace Lane
Wilcombe, Iowa 52515

Dear Mr. Green:

Thank _____ for _____ January 17 letter expressing
interest in the Englewood Golf Club. This letter will confirm
_____ plans for _____ meeting.

We understand that _____ company would like to reserve five
rooms at _____ facilities from September 10 to September 12.
Approximately 200 people will attend _____ meeting.

As _____ requested, _____ will provide five tables—one in
each room. All of the rooms have a microphone and a slide projector.
_____ will serve morning coffee and lunch on all three days.

If _____ have any questions or need to make any changes, please
contact _____ immediately.

We look forward to seeing _____ on September 10.

Sincerely,

Catherine Jones

Mrs. Catherine Jones

Meeting Planner

CJ/pr

Test Yourself

▶ *You are Ms. Turner's secretary. Follow her instructions and checklist. Write the letter on page 45.*

From the desk of
Jan Turner
MEETING PLANNER

Write a letter to Ms. White
and confirm our conversation
of 6/19/94.
Here's her card.

★ ★ ★ ★ ★ ★ ★ ★ ★ ★ ★

Ms. Ruth White
Director, Public Relations

STAR FURNITURE SUPPLIES
16 Darwin Road • Lexington, MA 02173
(617) 862-3904 • FAX (617) 862-3966

▲**rrowhead Conference Center**
412 Bellevue Lane
Brewster, Maryland 20906
(301) 594-5612 • Fax (301) 595-3317

CHECKLIST

Company: **Star Furniture Supplies**

Meeting Location: **Arrowhead Conference Center**

Date(s): Arrival Date **April 23**   Time: **9:00**

Departure Date **April 25**   Time: **5:00**

Number of people attending:

☐ 2-10   ☑ 51-100   ☐ Other _____

☐ 11-50   ☐ 101-150

Rooms Required: **5**

Audiovisual Requirements:

☑ Microphone   ☐ Tape recorder

☑ Slide projector   ☐ TV/VCR

Seating:

Tables **10 — 2 in each room**

Catering:

☑ Breakfast **(4/23+ 4/25)** ☑ Lunch   ☐ Reception

☑ Morning coffee   ☐ Afternoon coffee ☐ Dinner

Contact:

Name: **Ruth White**

Department: **Public Relations**

Telephone: **(617) 862-3904**   Fax: **(617) 862-3966**

▲rrowhead Conference Center
412 Bellevue Lane
Brewster, Maryland 20906
(301) 594-5612 • Fax (301) 595-3317

3A   Ordering Supplies

WORDS TO KNOW

(to) approve
back order
a bill
(to) bill
check
customer
fax
invoice
not in stock
(to) order
out of stock
payment
to prepare
price
(to) process
purchase order (P.O.)
(to) save
(to) ship
supplies
unfortunately
unit cost
vendor

▶ *Read this conversation.*

Yuki: Rosa, we need some supplies — like paper and paper clips.

Rosa: Write a memo to the Purchasing Department to order some, Yuki.

Yuki: Can't we just buy some supplies?

Rosa: No. We first have to write a memo to the Purchasing Department. They prepare a purchase order and send the purchase order to a vendor who sells office supplies.

Yuki: Then what?

Rosa: The vendor ships the supplies to you, and bills our company.

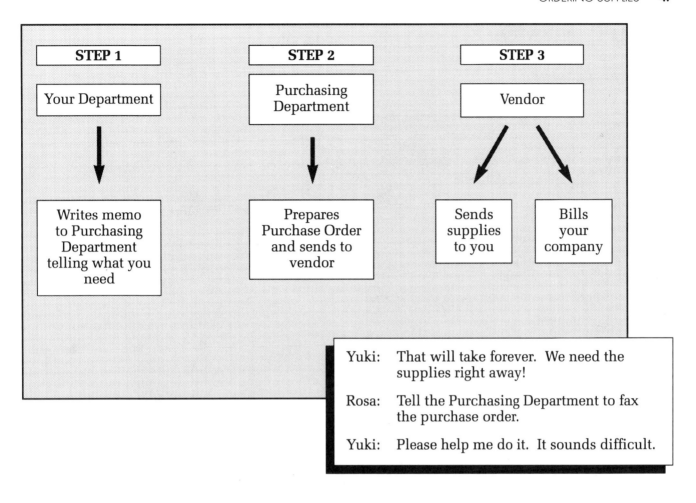

STEP 1	STEP 2	STEP 3

Your Department → Writes memo to Purchasing Department telling what you need

Purchasing Department → Prepares Purchase Order and sends to vendor

Vendor → Sends supplies to you / Bills your company

Yuki: That will take forever. We need the supplies right away!

Rosa: Tell the Purchasing Department to fax the purchase order.

Yuki: Please help me do it. It sounds difficult.

▶ *Complete each sentence with a word from the box.*

bills	ships
fax	supplies
order	vendor
purchase order	

Example:

Yuki wants to ____order____ pens and paper clips.

1. Rosa and Yuki need to order some _____ .

2. The Purchasing Department prepares a _____.

3. The _____ sells supplies.

4. The vendor _____ the supplies.

5. The purchase order will be sent by _____.

6. The vendor _____ the company for the supplies.

MODEL MEMO

▶*Look at this memo.*

MEMORANDUM

To: Peter Rekowski
                 Purchasing Department

From: Yuki Shibata   *YS*
                 Marketing Department
                 Ext. 545

Date: April 15, 1994

Subject: Supplies

Reference: Spring, 1994 Catalog
                 Executive Office Supplies
                 15 Watergate Plaza
                 New Orleans, LA 70116

Please prepare a purchase order ASAP for the following.

Item	Stock Number	Quantity	Unit Cost	Total Cost
Copier Paper (8½ x 11)	C 9837	4 ctns.	$54.95/2	$109.90
Pens, Black	P 4344	12 doz.	$22.45/doz.	$269.40
Pens, Red	P 5633	6 doz.	$22.45/doz.	$134.70
Paper Clips, large	C 4758	5 boxes	$1.95	$ 9.75

Subtotal	$523.75
Shipping/Handling 10%	$ 52.38
TOTAL	$576.13

Charge the total to the Marketing Department.

▶ *Circle the correct answer.*

1. Who wrote the memo?

   A. Yuki Shibata

   B. Peter Rekowski

2. Where does Peter Rekowski work?

   A. In the Marketing Department

   B. In the Purchasing Department

3. When was the memo written?

   A. April 15

   B. ASAP

4. What is the subject of the memo?

   A. Marketing

   B. Supplies

5. Who will prepare the Purchase Order?

   A. The Purchasing Department

   B. The Marketing Department

COMMON BUSINESS EXPRESSIONS

Shipping: Sending items from one place to another is called *shipping*. Items can be sent by mail, plane, truck, car, or ship.
Ship the copier paper to me by mail.
Send the copier paper to me by mail.

Handling: Items prepared for shipping are located, packed, and weighed. This preparation is called *handling*. Most businesses charge a fee for "Shipping and Handling." It is often a percentage of the total cost of the items.

BUSINESS STYLE: Body of an Order Memo

An order (memo order, purchase order, or order letter) must be complete. Do not leave out any details. It should answer these questions:

What: What do you want to order?

How: How much/how many do you want?

Who: Who will pay?

             Who will receive the order?

             Who will receive the bill?

When: When do you need your order?

▶ *Answer the questions. Use the Model Memo on page 48.*

1. What did Ms. Shibata order?

_____

2. How much/how many does she want?

_____

3. Who will pay?

_____

4. Who will receive the order?

_____

5. Who will receive the bill?

_____

6. When does she need the order?

_____

BUSINESS STYLE: Purchase Order

▶ *Read this purchase order. Peter Rekowski prepared it.*

A|E CONSTRUCTION
35 Hazel Wood Terrace
Logan, Utah 84321
801-561-3120

Purchase Order
Ship Prepaid • Add all delivery charges on invoice
Not to exceed $1000.00

Vendor: Executive Office Supplies
15 Watergate Plaza
New Orleans, LA 70116

Ship To: Yuki Shibata, Marketing Department
(use above address unless otherwise indicated)

Bill To: Purchasing Department
(use above address unless otherwise indicated)

Reference: P. O. 02-3450-6

Delivery Date: ASAP

Item	Stock Number	Quantity	Unit Cost	Total Cost
Copier Paper (8x10 1/2)	C 9837	4 ctns.	$54.95/2	$109.90
Pens, Black	P 4344	12 doz.	$22.45/doz.	$269.40
Pens, Red	P 5633	6 doz.	$22.45/doz.	$134.70
Paper Clips, large	C 4758	5 boxes	$1.95	$ 9.75
Subtotal				$523.75
Shipping/Handling 10%				$ 52.38
TOTAL				$576.13

Prepared by: *P. Rekowski*
Date prepared: *4/16/94*

Approved by: *Y. Shibato, Marketing*
Date approved: *4/16/94*

CC: Y. Shibata, Marketing / Accounting / Purchasing

▶ *Complete the answers.*

1. What supplies is Ms. Shibata ordering?

She is ordering four items: _____,

_____, _____,

and_____.

2. Which company is the vendor?

The Executive _____
company in New Orleans, Louisiana.

3. Which department will receive the bill?

The _____ department.

4. Which department will receive the supplies?

The _____ department.

5. How much is the total cost?

It's _____.

6. What is the unit cost for the paper?

It's _____.

7. How much is the shipping/handling?

It's _____.

MODEL COVER LETTER

▶ *Sometimes a cover letter is mailed with the purchase order. A cover letter describes what is enclosed in an envelope. Read this cover letter.*

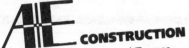

CONSTRUCTION
35 Hazel Wood Terrace
Logan, Utah 84321
(801) 561-3120
Fax: (801) 561-3388

April 17, 1994

Executive Office Supplies
15 Watergate Plaza
New Orleans, Louisiana 70116

Ref: P.O. 02-3450-6

Dear Sir or Madam:

The purchase order referenced above is enclosed.

Please process the order as soon as possible. If you have any questions, please contact me or Ms. Yuki Shibata, in the Marketing Department at (801) 561-3120.

Thank you for your prompt attention.

Sincerely,

Peter Rekowski

Peter Rekowski
Purchasing Assistant

Enclosure

▶ *Answer the questions.*

1. What is enclosed?

   A. A purchase order

   B. A check

2. When should the order be processed?

   A. ASAP

   B. Next year

3. How should Peter Rekowski be contacted?

   A. By phone

   B. By letter

4. Who does Mr. Rekowski work for?

   A. A&E Construction

   B. Executive Office Supplies

BUSINESS STYLE: Body of a Purchase Order Cover Letter

A cover letter generally has three parts.

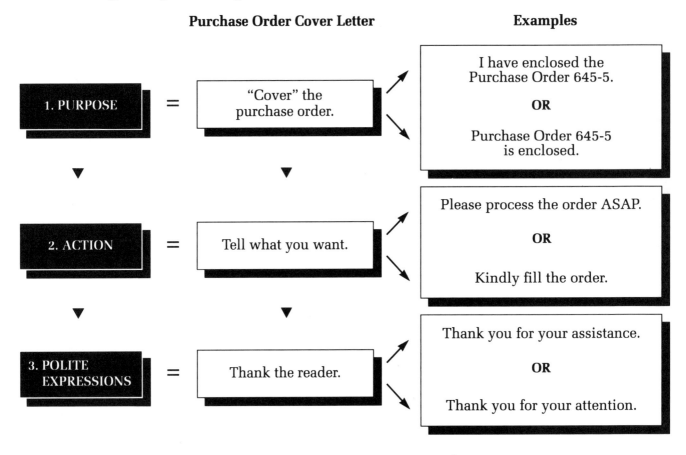

Purchase Order Cover Letter　　　　　　**Examples**

1. PURPOSE = "Cover" the purchase order.

I have enclosed the Purchase Order 645-5.

OR

Purchase Order 645-5 is enclosed.

2. ACTION = Tell what you want.

Please process the order ASAP.

OR

Kindly fill the order.

3. POLITE EXPRESSIONS = Thank the reader.

Thank you for your assistance.

OR

Thank you for your attention.

▶ *Look for these three parts in the Model Letter, page 51. Write the sentences.*

1. Purpose _____

2. Action _____

3. Polite Expressions _____

PUNCTUATION: Work Titles

Use a comma (,) to separate a person's name from his or her work title:

    Olivia Fraser, President

    David Wang, Chairman of the Board

    Tom Wilson, Director of Marketing

    Frederick Borg, Sales Manager

▶ *Put a comma in the correct place.*

1. Don Steele Chief Executive Officer

2. Katherine Gund Personnel Director

3. Manual Cabral Public Information Officer

4. Bruce Gelb File Clerk

5. Tina Dresner Office Manager

Memo Practice

▶ *Complete this memorandum with words from the box. Look at the Model Memo on page 48 for help.*

Desk	Price	Size
Ext.	Marketing	Department
SUBJECT	DATE	REFERENCE
Stock	Order	

From the desk of
M. WHITING
VP Marketing / K&F Consultants / Ext: 648

Ask the Purchasing Department to order the large desk from Olson's.

Olson's Furniture / 1993 Summer Catalog

EXECUTIVE DESK
Four side drawers, one center drawer, one file drawer.

Stock No.	Size	Sale Price
HN 31021	54" x 24"	$309.00
HN 31161	60" x 30"	$319.00

Shipping and Handling Included

▶ *Circle the correct answer.*

1. What does M. Whiting want?
   A. An executive desk
   B. A new telephone extension

2. What company sells the desk?
   A. Olson's Office Furniture
   B. K&F Consulting

3. Which desk does she want?
   A. The small one
   B. The large one

4. What is the Stock No. for the 60" x 30" desk?
   A. HN 31021
   B. HN 31161

5. What is the price of the large desk?
   A. $309.00
   B. $319.00

K+F Consultants   *MEMORANDUM*

TO: Purchasing _____

FROM: M. Whiting   *MW*

V.P. Marketing Department

_____ 648

_____ : June 25, 1993

_____ : Furniture Order

_____ : Olson's Office Furniture
                         Summer, 1993 Catalog
                         15 Watergate Plaza
                         New Orleans, LA 70116

Please prepare a purchase _____ ASAP for the following item.

Executive _____

_____ No.: HN 31161

_____ : 60"x30"

_____ : $319.00

Charge the total cost to the _____ Department.

MW/ec

Cover Letter Practice

K+F Consultants

394 West Philadelphia Avenue • Suite 392
Annapolis, Maryland 20896
(301) 581-2323   Fax: (301) 581-2222

Department Purchase Order
Ship Prepaid. Add all delivery charges on invoice.
Not to exceed $500.00

P.O. 650-218A

Vendor: OLSON'S OFFICE FURNITURE
                     15 Watergate Plaza
                     New Orleans, LA 70116

Delivery Date: ASAP

Ship To: M. Whiting, V.P. Marketing
                     (use above address unless otherwise indicated)

Bill To: Purchasing Department
                     (use above address unless otherwise indicated)

Item	Catalog No.	Quantity	Unit Cost	Total Cost
Executive Desk	HN 31161	1	319.00	$319.00
Additional charges: (Shipping/Handling)				00.00
Total				$319.00

Prepared by: *W. Rogers, Purchasing*
Date prepared: *June 26, 1993*

Approved by: *M. Whiting, Marketing*
Date approved: *June 27, 1993*

▶ *Correct the cover letter for the Purchase*
Order 650-218A. Look at the Model Letter
on page 51.

Type of Error	Number of Errors
Capitalization	5
Punctuation	5
Grammar	2
Spelling	2

K+F **Consultants**

394 West Philadelphia Avenue • Suite 392
Annapolis, Maryland 20896
(301) 581-2323   Fax: (301) 581-2222

1 June 26, 1993

2 Olson's Office Furniture
3 15 Watergate Plaza
4 new Orleans Louisiana 70116

5 Reference: P.O.650-218A

6 Deer sir or madam:

7 The purchase order referenced above are enclosed

8 please process the order as soon as possible If you has any
9 questions, please contact me or Ms. M. Whiting, Vice-President,
10 Marketing Department at (301) 581-2323

11 Thank you for your atention.

12 sincerely

13 *William Rogers*

14 W. Rodgers
15 Purchasing Assistant

16 Enclosure

Test Yourself: Memo

▶ *You work for Mr. R. Browning, the Vice President at Browning Developers. Write a memo for him to the Purchasing Department. Order 2 boxes of disks from the ad below. Look at the Model Memo on page 48.*

Spring Catalog

COMPUTER SUPPLY
6437 Wallford Avenue
Milbank, NY 10509

IBM USERS!
This sale is for you!
Quality diskettes at a very economical price. Buy a box of 10 and get one diskette FREE.
Box of 11, 5¼" DS/DD
Stock No. 4220
Sale Price $6.95/box of 11
No shipping or handling charges!

Browning Developers
1692 Main Street
Wakefield, MA 01880
617-246-0200

Test Yourself: Cover Letter

▶ *The Purchasing Department prepares Purchase Order 12-325X-1. Write a cover letter for the purchase order. Look at the model cover letter on page 51 for help.*

Browning Developers
1692 Main Street
Wakefield, MA 01880
617-246-0200

MODEL LETTER: Acknowledging an Order

EXECUTIVE OFFICE SUPPLIES
15 Watergate Plaza
New Orleans, Louisiana 70116
504-736-5223
Fax: 504-736-3123

April 22, 1994

Yuki Shibata
Marketing Department
A&E Construction
35 Hazel Wood Terrace
Logan, Utah 84321

Dear Ms. Shibata:

We received your Purchase Order 02-3450-6 on April 22, 1994. Unfortunately, the item below is not in stock:

Item No. P4344 Pens, black

We will backorder this item and ship it within three (3) weeks.

The rest of your order is being processed and will be shipped by Monday, April 25.

We appreciate your business and look forward to serving you in the future.

Sincerely yours,

John Peters
Shipping Clerk

▶ *Circle the correct answer.*

1. Where does John Peters work?
   A. A&E Construction
   B. Executive Office Supplies

2. Who ordered the supplies?
   A. John Peters
   B. Yuki Shibata

3. Who is the addressee?
   A. Executive Office Supplies
   B. Yuki Shibata

4. When was the letter sent?
   A. April 22   B. April 21

5. When was the P.O. received?
   A. April 22   B. April 25

6. Are the paper clips in stock?
   A. Yes   B. No

7. What is out of stock?
   A. Pens, Black, Item No. P4344
   B. Pens, Red, Item No. P5633

8. Are they on back order?
   A. Yes   B. No

9. When will they be sent?
   A. In 3 weeks
   B. In 2 weeks

10. When will the rest of the order be shipped?
    A. By Monday, April 25
    B. By April 23

BUSINESS STYLE: Body of a Letter Acknowledging an Order

An acknowledgement of an order generally has four parts.

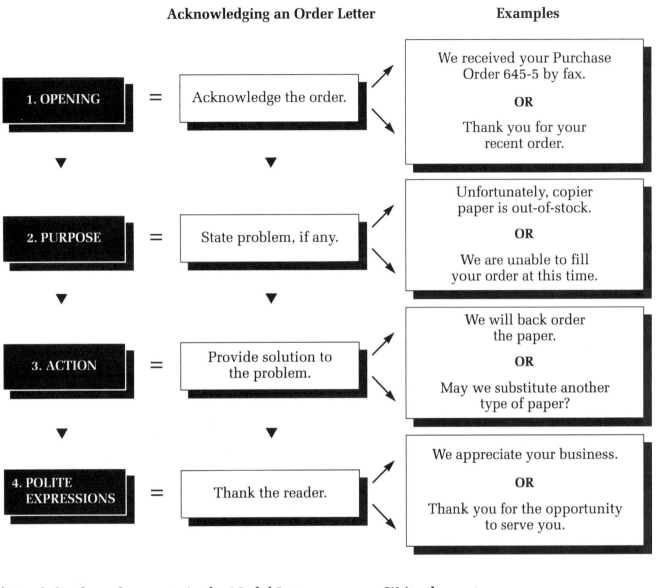

| Acknowledging an Order Letter | | Examples |

Acknowledging an Order Letter **Examples**

1. OPENING = Acknowledge the order.

We received your Purchase Order 645-5 by fax.

OR

Thank you for your recent order.

2. PURPOSE = State problem, if any.

Unfortunately, copier paper is out-of-stock.

OR

We are unable to fill your order at this time.

3. ACTION = Provide solution to the problem.

We will back order the paper.

OR

May we substitute another type of paper?

4. POLITE EXPRESSIONS = Thank the reader.

We appreciate your business.

OR

Thank you for the opportunity to serve you.

▶ *Look for these four parts in the Model Letter, page 58. Write the sentences.*

1. Opening _____

2. Purpose _____

3. Action _____

4. Polite Expressions _____

GRAMMAR: Sentence Fragments

A sentence fragment is only part of a sentence. Do NOT use sentence fragments in your letters.

Fragment

Need new desk.   No subject (*you* omitted)

Sentence

You need a new desk.

Fragment

You a new desk.   No verb (*need* omitted)

Sentence

You need a new desk.

Fragment

Because your old one is too small.   No main sentence (clause only)

Sentence

You need a new desk because your old one is too small.

▶ *Read the following sentences. Are they complete sentences or fragments? Circle the correct answer.*

Example:

If I can help you	Sentence	(Fragment)
If I can help you, please contact me.	(Sentence)	Fragment

1. We need a new chair.	Sentence	Fragment
We a new chair.	Sentence	Fragment
2. Sent the letter to the secretary.	Sentence	Fragment
The clerk sent the letter to the secretary.	Sentence	Fragment
3. Since we spoke on the telephone.	Sentence	Fragment
After our telephone conversation, I wrote you a letter.	Sentence	Fragment
4. Because the address was not correct, the letter was not delivered.	Sentence	Fragment
Because the address was not correct.	Sentence	Fragment
5. The invoice was paid last week.	Sentence	Fragment
The invoice last week.	Sentence	Fragment

Letter Practice 1

▶ *Correct the following letter.*

Type of Error	Number of Errors
Capitalization	5
Punctuation	5
Grammar	1
Spelling	2
Sentence Fragment	1

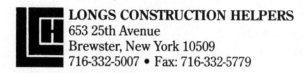

LONGS CONSTRUCTION HELPERS
653 25th Avenue
Brewster, New York 10509
716-332-5007 • Fax: 716-332-5779

1 January 3, 1994

2 Mrs. Ann Lawler
3 62 Chisolm Road
4 Carmel, New York 10513

5 Dear mrs Lawler'

6 We received your Purchase Order 456-99 on 12/11/93.
7 Unfortunately, the item below not in stock:

8   Item No. 45- BC Black Chair

9 We will back order this item and ship it by february 15,
10 1994?

11 The rest of your order is being processed and will be shipped
12 by january 20, 1994.

13 we appreciates your bussiness and look forward to serving you
14 in the future

15 sincerly yours

16 *Joseph Wilson*

17 Joseph Wilson
18 Shipping Clerk

Letter Practice 2

▶ *You are the Shipping Clerk for DeWitt's Office Supplies. It is your job to acknowledge orders. Write your reply using the information below and words from the box. Look at the Model Letter on page 58.*

Purchase Order No: *0092959*

Order Sent By: *Mr. R. Spruce*
Telephone Sales
2975 West 80th Drive,
Denver, CO 80221

Order Written On: *12/13/93*

Order Received On: *12/15/93*

Status of Order: *In process; to be shipped by 1/7/94*

Out-of-Stock Items: *Item No. C-342, conference desk*

New Ship Date: *2/28/94*

business	Desk	Order	you
Colorado	Drive	order	yours
Dear	February	processed	
December	Mr.	shipped	

DeWitt's Office Supplies
653 Fifth Avenue
Palm Springs, California 90087
818-656-5223 ■ Fax: 818-656-3123

December 20, 1993

_____ R. Spruce
Telephone Sales
2975 West 80th _____
Denver, _____ 80221

_____ Mr. Spruce:

We received your Purchase _____ 0092959 on _____
15, 1993. Unfortunately, the item below is not in stock:

   Item No. C-342 Conference _____

We will back _____ this item and ship it by
_____ 28, 1994.

The rest of your order is being _____ and will be
_____ by January 7, 1994.

We appreciate your _____ and look forward to serving
_____ in the future.

Sincerely _____,

_____
Shipping Clerk

DeW

Test Yourself

▶ *Read this information.*

Purchase Order No: B3-1229-69

Order Sent By: Mrs. S. Friedman
Secretarial College
123 Hori Loni
Honolulu, Hawaii 90073

Order Written On: 5/4/95

Order Received On: 5/8/95

Status of Order: In process; to be
shipped by 5/10/95

Out-of-Stock Items: item No. 90003
3½" diskettes

New Ship Date: 5/15/95

▶ *Write your own letter to acknowledge the order.*

DeWitt's Office Supplies
653 Fifth Avenue
Palm Springs, California 90087
818-656-5223 ■ Fax: 818-656-3123

4A Requesting Information

WORDS TO KNOW

(to) announce
announcement
article
available
brochure
camera
computer
dealer
first
front page
hesitate
inquiry
magazine
newspaper
page
section
sender
software
(to) wonder

▶ *Read this conversation.*

Jane: Jim, did you read today's newspaper?

Jim: Only the front page.

Jane: Read the article about the new camera.

Jim: What page is it on?

Jane: It's on the first page of the Business Section.

announces   newspaper
camera   page
first   wonders

▶ *Complete each sentence with a word from the box.*

Example:
Jane wondered if Jim had read today's _____ *newspaper* _____.

1. Jim had read only the front _____.

2. The article was about a new _____.

3. The article was on the _____ page of the Business section.

4. Click Camera Company _____ a new camera.

5. Jim _____ when the camera will be available.

MODEL LETTER: Requesting Information

▶*Jane writes a letter to the Click Camera Company.*

Bay State Magazine
300 Commonwealth Avenue
Boston, Massachusetts 02188
617-798-5556
FAX 617-798-0565

April 5, 1994

Public Information Department
Click Camera Company
1000 Riverview Boulevard
New York, New York 10010

Dear Sir or Madam:

In the April 4, 1994 Boston Daily News I read about your new camera, the XL-Lite. Since I am a photographer with Bay State Magazine, it is important that I know about new cameras.

Would you please send me information on the camera? I would like to know when the camera will be available and how much it will cost.

Thank you for your attention. I look forward to your reply.

Sincerely yours,

Jane Wilson
Photo Department

▶ *Circle the correct answer.*

1. Jane wrote her letter on

   A. April 4.   B April 5.

2. Jane's job is with the

   A. Bay State Magazine.

   B. Click Camera Company.

3. The Click Camera Company is located in

   A. Massachusetts.

   B. New York.

4. The number 10010 is the zip code of the

   A. sender.   B. addressee.

5. Jane wants Click Camera Company to send

   A. information.

   B. a camera.

6. The paragraphs of this letter are

   A. indented.

   B. not indented.

PUNCTUATION: Direct and Indirect Questions

Use a question mark (?) at the end of a direct question.

> When will the camera be available?

> What will the camera cost?

Use a period (.) at the end of a sentence that includes an indirect question.

> Jim wonders when the camera will be available.

> They wonder what the camera will cost.

▶ *Circle the correct punctuation.*

Example:

When can we get the information   (?)   .

1. When did Jane write the letter   ?   .

2. Jim wonders when Jane wrote the letter   ?   .

3. How much does the camera cost   ?   .

4. I'd like to know how the camera works   ?   .

5. Jane and Jim wonder what kind of camera it is   ?   .

6. Did you read the newspaper   ?   .

7. She doesn't know how much it costs   ?   .

8. Do we need a computer   ?   .

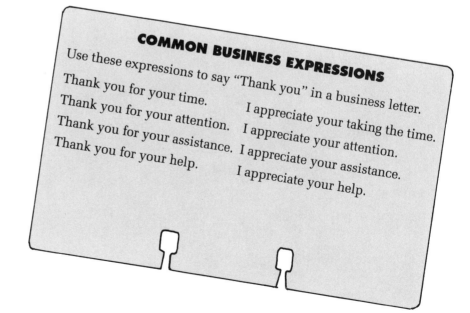

COMMON BUSINESS EXPRESSIONS

Use these expressions to say "Thank you" in a business letter.

Thank you for your time.

Thank you for your attention.

Thank you for your assistance.

Thank you for your help.

I appreciate your taking the time.

I appreciate your attention.

I appreciate your assistance.

I appreciate your help.

BUSINESS STYLE: Body of a Letter Requesting Information

A letter requesting information generally has four parts.

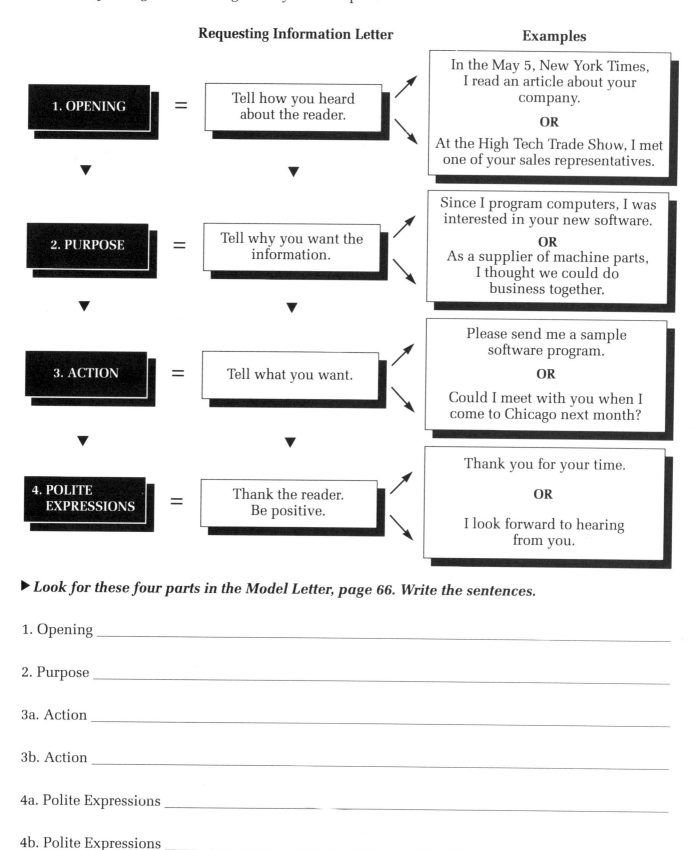

Requesting Information Letter   **Examples**

1. OPENING = Tell how you heard about the reader.

> In the May 5, New York Times, I read an article about your company.
>
> **OR**
>
> At the High Tech Trade Show, I met one of your sales representatives.

2. PURPOSE = Tell why you want the information.

> Since I program computers, I was interested in your new software.
>
> **OR**
>
> As a supplier of machine parts, I thought we could do business together.

3. ACTION = Tell what you want.

> Please send me a sample software program.
>
> **OR**
>
> Could I meet with you when I come to Chicago next month?

4. POLITE EXPRESSIONS = Thank the reader. Be positive.

> Thank you for your time.
>
> **OR**
>
> I look forward to hearing from you.

▶ *Look for these four parts in the Model Letter, page 66. Write the sentences.*

1. Opening _____

2. Purpose _____

3a. Action _____

3b. Action _____

4a. Polite Expressions _____

4b. Polite Expressions _____

GRAMMAR: Prepositions of Place

Prepositions of place tell "where."

In

Where are the envelopes?

The envelopes are *in* the desk drawer.

On

Where is the Computer Department?

The Computer Department is *on* the fifth floor.

At

Where do you work?

I work *at* the Embassy Camera Shop.

From (one place) **to** (another place)

Where does the train go?

The train goes *from* New York *to* Rochester.

> ▶ *Complete each sentence with a word from the box.*

at	on
from	to
in	

1. The article was _____ the Daily News.

2. The article was _____ the front page of the newspaper.

3. Jamie works _____ Bay State Magazine.

4. Our office is _____ the tenth floor.

5. We sent the fax _____ Tokyo.

6. I received a fax _____ Seoul.

7. The announcement was _____ today's newspaper.

8. The advertisement was _____ the last page.

9. I live _____ Park Avenue.

10. I live _____ 640 Park Avenue.

BUSINESS STYLE: Commands or Requests

In business letters, use polite expressions. You should make "requests" instead of "commands."

Command: Send me the information.
Request: If you have time, could you please answer this today?

Command: Send the package next week.
Request: If it is possible, please send the package next week.

Polite expressions of request:

Would you please....   Would you possibly...?

If it isn't too much trouble, ...   I would be grateful if you could....

If you have the time, ...   I would be grateful if you would....

If it is possible, could you ...?   May I ask you to...?

If it is possible, would you ...?   I would appreciate it if you could....

Could you possibly...?   I would appreciate it if you would....

▶ *Rewrite each command and make it a polite request.*

Example:

Call me later.

Could you possibly _____call me later_____?

1. Stop sending me catalogs.

   I would appreciate it if you would _____.

2. Process the order right away.

   Would you please _____?

3. Give me the information I need.

   I would be grateful if you could _____.

4. Answer my letter immediately.

   If you have the time, _____?

5. Send me your response right away.

   If it is possible, _____?

Letter Practice 1

▶ *Look at the following vendor list for computer software.*

Software Magazine
Vendor List
Educational Software Suppliers

Company	Computer
EduLink	IBM
Route 128	
Stoneham, MA 02167	
MathDiscs	Apple
143 Salt Drive	
Cupertino, CA 22128	
Intel	IBM
381 Park Avenue	
New York, NY 1016	
Schoolware, Inc.	IBM, Apple
6767 Westwood	
Los Angeles, CA 90024	

Educational Software Suppliers May 20, 1993

▶ *Correct Dr. Barth's letter. Refer to the Model Letter on page 66.*

Type of Error	Number of Errors
Capitalization	14
Punctuation	9
Command vs. Polite Request	2

Foreign Language Institute
555 Deer Run Lane
Aurora, CO 80014
303-632-8404
FAX 303-632-1541

1 august 21 1994

2 Sandberg Educational, inc
3 orchard Ridge Corporate Park
4 building Two, Fields lane
5 brewster, ny 10509

6 Dear sir or madam

7   in the winter issue of Multimedia News we read that your
8 company sells language laboratories   our school needs a new
9 language laboratory and we are looking for the best equipment

10   Send us information on your laboratories Would you also
11 include a price list and ordering information.

12   thank you for your assistance I look forward to hearing
13 from you

14 sincerely yours

15 *John Barth*

16 John Barth
17 dean of Students

Letter Practice 2

▶ *Use the same vendor list and the words from the box to write a letter to another software company. Refer to the Model Letter on page 66.*

and	computers	information	Sincerely
are	educational	looking	Sir
attention	for	Madam	Thank
August	forward	Our	us
company	In	please	Would
computer	include	products	

Mount Morsey High School
8547 16th Street
Des Moines, Iowa 53500
515-821-6871

_____ 10, 1993

_____

_____

_____

Dear _____ or _____:

_____ the August issue of Software Magazine, we read that your

_____ sells _____ software. _____

teachers _____ always _____ for new software

_____ for IBM _____

_____ you_____ send _____ a catalog of

your _____ products? Would you also _____ a price

list _____ ordering _____?

_____ you _____ your _____. I look

_____ to hearing from you.

_____ yours,

_____

Test Yourself

▶ *Write your own form letter to another software company, to a book company, etc. Ask for a product that interests you. Remember to use How, Why, What, and Thanks.*

MODEL LETTER: Providing Information

▶ *Read the following letter.*

CLICK CAMERA COMPANY
1000 Riverview Boulevard
New York, New York 10010
212-589-2121 • FAX 212-588-9542

April 10, 1993

Jane Wilson
Bay State Magazine
300 Commonwealth Avenue
Boston, Massachusetts 02188

Dear Ms. Wilson:

Thank you for your letter of April 5, 1993 expressing interest in Click Camera's new camera, the XL-Lite.

The camera will be available this December, and the cost will be approximately three hundred and fifty dollars ($350.00).

I have enclosed a brochure on the camera. If you have any questions, please do not hesitate to contact us or your local Click Camera dealer.

Again, thank you for your inquiry.

Sincerely yours,

Helen Dodge

Helen Dodge
Customer Service

Enclosure

▶ *Circle the correct answer.*

1. Ms. Dodge works for
   A. Click Camera Company.
   B. Bay State Magazine.

2. When was this letter written?
   A. April 10   B. April 5

3. What is Ms. Dodge sending to Ms. Wilson?
   A. a camera
   B. information

4. What is another word for "inquiry?"
   A. request   B. brochure

5. What will Helen put on the envelope?
   A. Ms. Jane Wilson
      Bay State Magazine
      300 Commonwealth Avenue
      Boston, MA 02188
   B. Ms. Helen Dodge
      Click Camera Company
      1000 Riverview Boulevard
      New York, New York 10010

6. The paragraphs are
   A. indented.
   B. not indented.

BUSINESS STYLE: Body of a Form Letter Providing Information

A letter providing information generally has four parts.

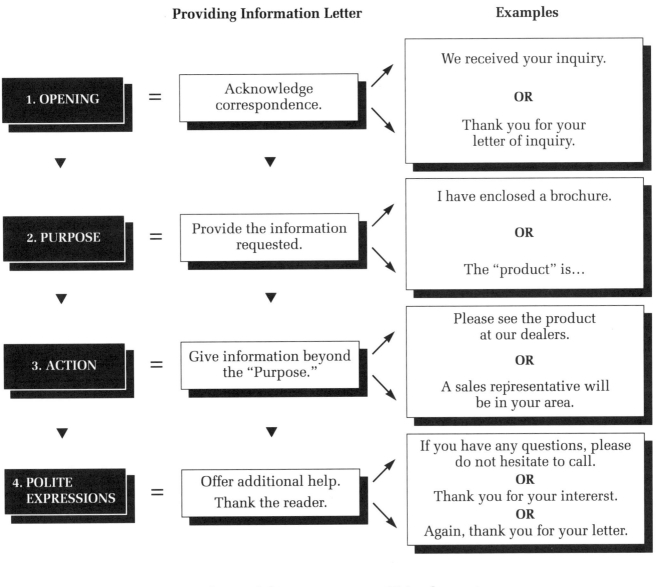

| Providing Information Letter | Examples |

▶ *Look for these four parts in the Model Letter, page 74. Write the sentences.*

1. Opening _____

2. Purpose _____

3. Action _____

4. Polite Expressions _____

PUNCTUATION: Possession

One use for the apostrophe is to show possession.
If the noun does not end in s, add 's:

the file of the clerk	the clerk's file
the number of the messenger	the messenger's number

If the noun ends in s, add only the apostrophe (') :

the meeting of the managers	the managers' meeting
the names of the secretaries	the secretaries' names

▶ *Rewrite the following to show possession.*

Example:

the letter of the clerk   *the clerk's letter*

1. the addresses of the employees

2. the catalog of the vendor

3. policies of all the companies

4. the desk of the secretary

5. the job of the manager

6. the offices of the vice presidents

7. the products of the company

8. the meeting of the marketing department

9. the coffee break of the clerks

10. the vacation of the chairman

BUSINESS STYLE: Asking for Clarification

When writing numbers in a business letter, it is a good idea to repeat the number in words. This redundancy helps clarify the information.

Quantity	Letter Style
5 boxes	five (5) boxes
10 gross	ten (10) gross

Amount	Letter Style
$6.42	six dollars and forty-two cents ($6.42)
$3,500	three thousand, five hundred dollars ($3,500)

▶ *You received letters with unclear numbers. Ask for clarification. Write the word first, followed by the number in parentheses.*

Example:

Unclear: Please send us five (15) cartons of envelopes.
                     word   number

Clear: Do you want fifteen (15) cartons of envelopes or five (5) cartons of envelopes?
                     word   number   **word   number**

1. *Unclear:* The total is thirty-two dollars $3.20.

   Clear: Is the total thirty-two dollars ($_____) or _____dollars and

                     _____cents ($3.20)?

2. *Unclear:* We will need six (60) boxes of copier paper.

   Clear: Do you want six (_____) boxes of copier paper or sixty (_____)
                     boxes of copier paper?

3. *Unclear:* The shipping cost is eleven percent (10%) of the total.

   Clear: Is the shipping cost _____ percent (_____%) of the total or

                     _____ percent (_____%)?

4. *Unclear:* Please send us one (100) dozen pens.

   Clear: Do you need _____ (_____) dozen pens or _____

                     (_____) dozen pens?

PUNCTUATION: Conjunctions

Use a comma to separate two sentences linked by a conjunction. The comma always comes before the conjunction.

Conjunctions: *but, and, or, nor, yet*

> The brochure is enclosed, *and* a dealer will contact you soon.

> We apologize for the delay, *but* your letter was misplaced.

▶ *Combine the following sentences into one sentence. Use the correct conjunction.*

1. *but*   *or*

   I received your catalog. The price list was not enclosed.

   _____

   _____

2. *yet*   *or*

   We will call you. You will receive a letter from us.

   _____

   _____

3. *but*   *nor*

   The package did not arrive. The invoice did.

   _____

   _____

4. *or*   *but*

   The letter was ready. The mail carrier was late.

   _____

   _____

Form Letter Practice 1

A form letter is a letter sent to many different people. The body of the letter is the same, but the inside address and greeting change. Information such as dates may change.

▶ *Ms. Dodge received many letters of inquiry. She asks you to type a form letter to reply to the letters requesting information. Correct her form letter. Use the Model Letter on page 74 for help.*

Type of Error	Number of Errors
Capitalization	11
Punctuation	7
Word order	1
Grammar	2
Spelling	1

INFORMATION REQUEST FOLLOW UP

Rec'd: 7/25/93

Reply Sent: 7/26/93

Name: *Mrs. Ida Roth*

Address: *9616 Jefferson Street*

City/State/Zip: *St. Louis Park, Minnesota 55416*

Product: X *L-Lite*

CLICK CAMERA COMPANY
1000 Riverview Boulevard
New York, New York 10010
212-589-2121 • FAX 212-588-9542

1 1993 July 26

2 ms. ida roth
3 616 jefferson Sttreet
4 St. Louis Park, minnesota: 55416

5 Ms. roth?
6 Dear

7 thank you for your letter of July 22 1993 expressing interest in Click
8 Camera s new camera, the XL-Lite.

9 The camera will be available this december and the cost will be
10 approximately three hundred and fifty dollars ($350.00).

11 I have enclosed a brochure on the camera. If you has any questions,
12 please do not hesitate to contact us or your local Click Camera dealer?

13 again, thanks you for your inquiry?

14 Sincerely yours

15 *Helen Dodge*

16 Helen Dodge
17 customer Service

18 enclosure

Form Letter Practice 2

▶ *Complete the form letter. Use the words from the box and the Information Request form for help.*

available	inquiry	thank
enclosed	not	you
interest	please	

INFORMATION REQUEST FOLLOW UP

Rec'd: *July 24, 1993*

Reply Sent:

Name: *Mrs. May Carter*

Address: *4015 22nd Street*

City/State/Zip: *Honolulu, Hawaii 96822*

Product: *XL-Lite*

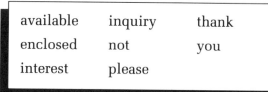

CLICK CAMERA COMPANY
1000 Riverview Boulevard
New York, New York 10010
212-589-2121 • FAX 212-588-9542

_____

Mrs. May Carter
4015 22nd Street
Honolulu, Hawaii 96822

Dear: _____:

Thank _____ for your letter of _____ expressing
_____ in Click Camera's new camera, the XL-Lite.

The camera will be _____ this December, and the cost will be
approximately three hundred and fifty dollars ($350.00).

I have _____ a brochure on the camera. If you have any
questions, _____ do _____ hesitate to contact
us or your local Click Camera dealer.

Again, _____ you for your _____

Sincerely yours,

Helen Dodge

Helen Dodge
Customer Service

Enclosure

Test Yourself

▶ *NEC has received many requests for information about its computers. Write a reply from NEC for Mr. Menice.*

NEC
TECH 2000 BUILDING
800 K STREET, NW
WASHINGTON, D.C. 20001
202-574-0102
FAX 202-574-9866

INFORMATION REQUEST FOLLOW UP

Inquiry Date: August 21, 1994

Contact: John Barth, Ph.D.

Title: Dean of Students

Company/Institution: Foreign Language Institute

Address: 555 Deer Run Lane
Aurora, CO 80014

Reply sent: August 28, 1994

WORDS TO KNOW

adjustment
apologetic
(to) apologize
apology
claim
cooperation
credit
(to) credit
error
inconvenience
(to) happen
overnight mail
refund
regret
replacement
shipment

▶ *Read this conversation.*

Jeff: Are these the new training manuals?

Holly: Yes, but they're the wrong ones.

Jeff: Do you still have the original purchase order?

Holly: Yes. We had the right stock numbers. They sent the wrong manuals.

PURCHASE ORDER
NO. R-6632

W

WILSON & COMPANY, Ltd.
51 Wimbleton Road
Toronto, Ontario M4D 2V8 Canada
(416) 888-4444
FAX (416) 999-4443

SHIP TO: (Use above address unless otherwise indicated below.)

TO: New Tech Publications
454 Liberty Road
Philadelphia, PA 19148

QUANTITY	DESCRIPTION	STOCK NO.	UNIT COST	TOTAL COST
2	Training Manuals	TM-0053-3 TM-0056-7	12.50	25.00 S/H 3.75

Jeff: Fax a claim letter. We need these manuals right away!

Holly: I was going to send it by overnight mail, but I'll fax it.

claim	overnight mail
credit	refund
error	replacement

▶ *Complete each sentence with a word from the box.*

Example:

Holly wrote a _____ *claim* _____ letter to the company.

1. The company could send a _____ — the correct manuals.

2. Or the company could send a _____ in the form of cash or a check.

3. The company could also _____ Holly's account for the manuals.

4. Shippers should apologize when they make an _____.

5. Holly sent the letter by fax not by _____.

MODEL LETTER: Claim Letter

▶ *Read the letter.*

▶ *Circle the correct answer.*

WILSON & COMPANY, Ltd.
51 Wimbleton Road
Toronto, Ontario M4D 2V8 Canada
(416) 888-4444
FAX (416) 999-4443

May 7, 1994

Mr. Roland Fischer, Manager
New Tech Publications
454 Liberty Road
Philadelphia, Pennsylvania 19148

Dear Mr. Fischer:

On April 1, I ordered manuals numbers TM-0053-3 and TM-0056-7. On May 7, I received two copies of manual number TM-003553.

I am returning — under separate cover — the two training manuals.

Please send me the two (2) manuals. Also please correct my account-— No.594-OC. The invoice was for thirty-two dollars and fifty cents ($32.50), it should be (twenty-eight dollars and seventy-five cents ($28.75).

Thank you for your assistance.

Cordially yours,

Holly Park

Holly Park

1. Holly wrote this letter to place an order.

   A. Yes   B. No

2. Ms. Park is returning two manuals to New Tech Publications.

   A. Yes   B. No

3. Ms. Park wants a refund.

   A. Yes   B. No

4. Did Ms. Park enclose a check?

   A. Yes   B. No

5. Has Ms. Park been billed?

   A. Yes   B. No

6. The catalog numbers are TM-0053-3 and TM-0056-7.

   A. Yes   B. No

7. There was an error on the invoice.

   A. Yes   B. No

COMMON BUSINESS EXPRESSIONS

Sent under separate cover = Sent separately

Items that cannot fit in an envelope with a letter are put in a box and sent separately. The letter explains the box is sent under separate cover.

BUSINESS STYLE: Body of a Claim Letter

A claim letter generally has four parts.

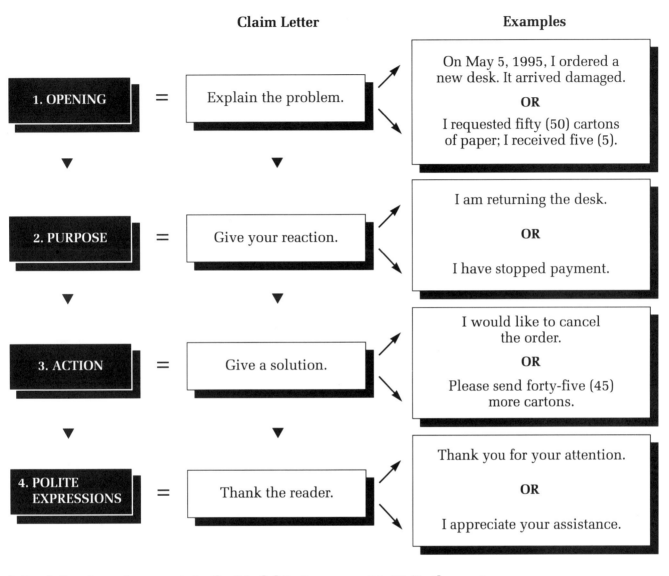

Claim Letter	Examples

1. OPENING = Explain the problem.

On May 5, 1995, I ordered a new desk. It arrived damaged.

OR

I requested fifty (50) cartons of paper; I received five (5).

2. PURPOSE = Give your reaction.

I am returning the desk.

OR

I have stopped payment.

3. ACTION = Give a solution.

I would like to cancel the order.

OR

Please send forty-five (45) more cartons.

4. POLITE EXPRESSIONS = Thank the reader.

Thank you for your attention.

OR

I appreciate your assistance.

▶ *Look for these four parts in the Model Letter, page 84. Write the sentences.*

1. Opening _____

2. Purpose _____

3. Action _____

4. Polite Expressions _____

PUNCTUATION: Adding Information

Dashes (—) are used in place of commas, colons, and parentheses to add information:

> Thanksgiving — a national holiday in the United States— is celebrated in November.

Dashes are also used to show emphasis:

> The letter contained errors—a great many errors—that the typist made.

Dashes are also used to set off lists:

> The letter which gave the following information — the date, the time and the cost of the shipment—was delivered by messenger.

Dashes are written as a long line; they are typed by typing the hyphen key twice. (--)

▶ *Rewrite the sentences. Use a dash.*

Example:

This book on correspondence (letters, faxes, and memos) is a great reference.

This book on correspondence—letters, faxes, and memos— is a great reference.

1. Four employees (all in the accounting department) were given raises.

_____

_____

2. The final report (the one with so many changes) was finished on Friday.

_____

_____

3. The entire contents of the package was damaged: stationery, envelopes, and notebooks.

_____

_____

4. All of the supplies were lost during shipping: the books, the paper, the tapes, and the disks.

_____

_____

BUSINESS STYLE: Formal or Informal

Contractions are generally not used in business letters, because they give a less formal tone to the letter.

Formal: Do not send payment without the invoice.

Informal: Don't send payment without the invoice.

Formal: We cannot complete the purchase order.

Informal: We can't complete the purchase order.

▶ *Circle the contractions. Rewrite the following sentences. Make them formal.*

Example:

(Don't) forget to add 10% for shipping and handling.

Do not forget to add 10% for shipping and handling.

1. Please don't send any brochures.

2. We can't process the order.

3. We won't ship the supplies without a purchase order.

4. The order wasn't received last week.

5. The item isn't in stock.

GRAMMAR: Prepositions

Some verbs are followed by a preposition. These are called two-word verbs.

▶ *Rewrite the letter below on your own paper. Replace the single-word verbs with two-word verbs.*

arrived on	=	came	billed for	=	charged
asked for	=	ordered	sending back	=	returning

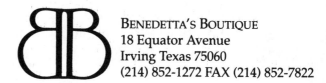

BENEDETTA'S BOUTIQUE
18 Equator Avenue
Irving Texas 75060
(214) 852-1272 FAX (214) 852-7822

1 November 18, 1993

2 Mr. Andrew Dale
3 Grand Office Supplies
4 457 Broome Street
5 Boulder, Colorado 80306

6 Dear Mr. Dale:

7 On October 15, I ordered two (2) cartons of size fifteen (15)
8 envelopes. On November 1, I received two (2) cartons of size
9 ten (10) envelopes.

10 I am returning — under separate cover — two cartons of
11 these envelopes.

12 Please send me the two (2) cartons. Also, please correct my
13 account — No. 6032. On the invoice I was charged (eighty-five
14 dollars) $85.00; It should be (fifty-eight dollars) $58.00.

15 Thank you for your assistance.

16 Sincerely yours,

17 *Carol Scanner*

18 Carol Scanner
19 President

20 CS/pt

Letter Practice 1

▶ *Correct the errors. Refer to the Model Letter on page 84.*

Type of Error	Number of Errors
Capitalization	7
Punctuation	3
Spelling	2
Word order	1
Style: Formal/Informal	2

WILSON & COMPANY, Ltd.
51 Wimbleton Road
Toronto, Ontario M4D 2V8 Canada
(416) 888-4444
FAX (416) 999-4443

1 May 3, 1994

2 SUPPLIES LIMITED

3 Box 49

4 Oakville, Ontario L6J 7K1

5 Canada

6 sir or Dear madam,

7 this morning I received a carton of computer printout

8 paper — Stock No. CP4-9. The paper is useless — the carton

9 was damaged and wet. I'm returning it under separate cover.

10 We'd like a replacement as soon as possible

11 Please call me if there are any questions? thank your

12 for your cooperation.

13 cordialy yours,

14 *Holly Park*

15 holly park

Letter Practice 2

▶ *Read the information on the memo pad below.*

▶ *Complete the sentences. Use the information on the memo pad and the words from the box.*

Avenue	November	work
like	possible	you
model	TOOLS	your

THINGS TO DO TODAY

From the desk of: **Constance Monahan**

11/5/94
Write a letter to:
TECH TOOLS, INC.
3593 Johnson Ave., Houston, TX 78646
Explain to them that yesterday
I received a calculator—
Odysseus model #AL-54 — that
doesn't work.
I want a replacement ASAP

A&P ACCOUNTANTS
4563 Presley Avenue
Memphis, Tennessee 50647
(901)-231-0571
FAX (901) 231-6642

November 5, 1994

TECH _____ , Inc.

3553 Johnson _____

_____ , Texas _____

Dear Sir or Madam:

On _____ 4, 19 _____ , I received the
calculator I ordered.

I am returning — under separate cover — the calculator, Odysseus
_____ # AL-54 because it doesn't _____ .

I would _____ a replacement as soon as _____ .

Thank _____ for _____ cooperation.

Cordially yours,

Constance Monahan

Constance Monahan

Enclosure

CM/_____

Test Yourself

▶ *Write a claim letter. Here are some ideas.*

- Write to a company that sent you a poor product.
- Write to a company that sent you a damaged product.
- Write to a company that sent you the wrong product.
- Write to a company that gives poor service.
- Write to a restaurant about the service or food.

MODEL FAX: Adjustment Letter

▶ *Look at the following letter. It was sent by fax to Ms. Park.*

New Tech Publications
454 Liberty Road
Philadelphia, PA 19145
(215) 652-8800 • FAX (215) 652-8181

FAX COVER SHEET

To: Holly Park

New Tech Publications
454 Liberty Road
Philadelphia, PA 19145
(215) 652-8800 • FAX (215) 652-8181

May 27, 1994

Holly Park
Wilson & Company, Ltd.
51 Wimbleton Road
Toronto, Ontario M4D 2V8
Canada

Dear Ms. Park:

Thank you for your letter which we received on May 20. We apologize for the error.

Two manuals— #TM-0053-3 and #TM-0056-7 — will be sent by overnight mail.

You will receive them tomorrow. A new invoice (No. 5430) for $28.20 is enclosed.

Again we regret the error and apologize for any inconvenience. We look forward to serving you in the future.

Sincerely yours,

Roland Fischer

Roland Fischer
Supply Chief

Enclosure: Invoice No. 5430

▶ *Circle the correct answer.*

1. Who wrote the claim letter?
   A. Mr. Fischer   B. Ms. Park

2. Who wrote the adjustment letter?
   A. Mr. Fischer   B. Ms. Park

3. What was the problem?
   A. The wrong manuals were sent.
   B. The manuals did not arrive.

4. How does Mr. Fischer help?
   A. He cancels the order.
   B. He ships the items immediately.

5. What describes Mr. Fischer?
   A. Apologetic   B. Angry

6. How was the invoice sent?
   A. With the manuals
   B. With the letter

7. In which paragraph is there an apology?
   A. Paragraph 1   B. Paragraph 2

8. In which other paragraph is there an apology?
   A. Paragraph 3   B. Paragraph 4

GOOD BUSINESS NOTE

In some companies, the enclosures are listed.

BUSINESS STYLE: Body of an Adjustment Letter

The body of an adjustment letter generally has four parts.

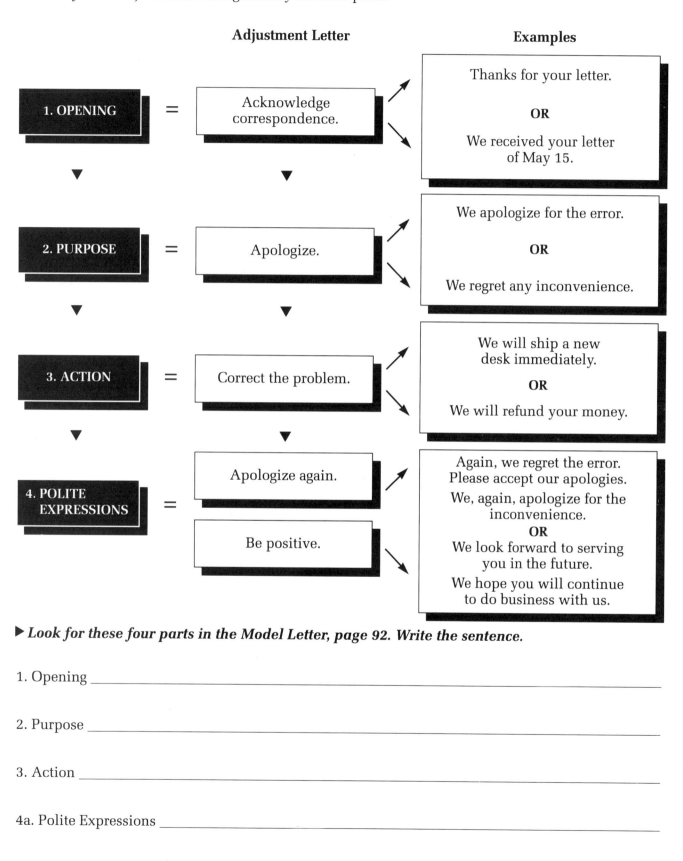

Adjustment Letter		Examples
1. OPENING =	Acknowledge correspondence.	Thanks for your letter. **OR** We received your letter of May 15.
2. PURPOSE =	Apologize.	We apologize for the error. **OR** We regret any inconvenience.
3. ACTION =	Correct the problem.	We will ship a new desk immediately. **OR** We will refund your money.
4. POLITE EXPRESSIONS =	Apologize again. / Be positive.	Again, we regret the error. Please accept our apologies. We, again, apologize for the inconvenience. **OR** We look forward to serving you in the future. We hope you will continue to do business with us.

▶ *Look for these four parts in the Model Letter, page 92. Write the sentence.*

1. Opening _____

2. Purpose _____

3. Action _____

4a. Polite Expressions _____

4b. Polite Expressions _____

BUSINESS STYLE: Adjustment Letter Actions

An adjustment letter may have three possible actions:

a refund	=	You receive your money back.
a replacement	=	You receive the same item without a problem.
a credit	=	You receive a store credit and can take other items in the store within the credit limit.

▶ *Write whether the action is a refund, a replacement, or a credit.*

Example:

refund You will receive a refund check in the mail.

1. _____ Please return the umbrella and pick out a new one.

2. _____ $45.00 has been credited to your account.

3. _____ The money will be refunded tomorrow.

4. _____ You are invited to choose another color.

5. _____ We are out of that item, but please select something else from our store.

Notice in the model letter that the author begins with an apology, suggests an action, and ends with an apology.

▶ *Write whether the action is an apology or an action.*

Example:

action You may exchange the item at your convenience.

GOOD BUSINESS NOTE
The customer is always right!

1. _____ I regret any inconvenience.

2. _____ You will receive a refund for 35 cents.

3. _____ Please accept a free ticket to anywhere in the world.

4. _____ I am sorry our umbrella did not open properly.

5. _____ A new fax machine will be sent to you.

GRAMMAR: Infinitives

The infinitive is the base form of the verb. It is introduced by *to*:

to speak   to see   to read   to write

▶ *Underline the verb. Then write the infinitive form.*

Example:

She <u>spoke </u>to her supervisor.   ___to speak___

1. The secretary typed the letter this morning.   _____

2. The manager chose the best copier.   _____

3. I wrote the memo this morning.   _____

4. They sent the shipment out yesterday.   _____

5. We found the invoice.   _____

To make an infinitive negative, put *not* before the infinitive.

▶ *Underline the infinitive. Then write the negative infinitive form.*

Example:

I told him <u>to send</u> the letter.   ___not to send___

1. We advised them to send a refund.   _____

2. Tell him to ask for full payment.   _____

3. I prefer to arrive early.   _____

4. He decided to go.   _____

5. They told us to miss the meeting.   _____

Use infinitives after certain verbs in American English.

The employees hope to finish the project soon.

Some of these verbs are:

agree	choose
expect	want
hope	learn
need	plan
promise	want

▶ *Combine the sentences. Use the infinitive form.*

get   *apologize*

1. They intend _____ more business by advertising.

2. We want _____ for our error.

send   *leave*

3. Our clients need _____ at 2:00.

4. The manager agrees _____ a refund.

fix   *know*

5. Mr. Banks promises _____ the problem.

6. We expect _____ the answer by tomorrow.

install   *hear*

7. I hope _____ from the client soon.

8. They plan _____ the new computer system today.

Fax Practice 1

▶ *Correct the following letter that was sent by fax.*

Type of Error	Number of Errors
Capitalization	4
No space	2
Omitted words	2
Repetition	2
Pronoun agreement	1
Infinitive	1

New Tech Publications
454 Liberty Road
Philadelphia, PA 19145
(215) 652-8800 • FAX (215) 652-8181

FAX COVER SHEET

DATE: May 27, 1994

TO: Holly Park

CO.: Wilson & Company

FROM: Roland Fischer

SUBJECT: Manuals #TM-0053
#TM-11356-7

PAGES: This plus one

New Tech Publications
454 Liberty Road
Philadelphia, PA 19145
TEL:215-652-8800 • FAX: 215-652-8181

1 May 27, 1994

2 Holly Park
3 Wilson & Company
4 51 Wimbleton Road
5 Toronto, Ontario M4D 2V8
6 Canada

7 Dear Ms. Park:

8 In response toyour letter of May 20, we apologize
9 the the error in your shipment. We apologize for
10 the error in your shipment.

11 To correct error, the new manuals will be to send by
12 overnight mail. you should receive it tomorrow.

13 We hope we do not cause you any further
14 inconvenience.

15 Sincerely

17 Roland Fischer

18 RF/kk

Fax Practice 2

▶ *Read the following messages and prepare the reply. Use the words from the box.*

apologize	July	sorry
Brown	overnight	you
Dr.	receive	
inconvenience	shipment	

TELEPHONE MESSAGE

FOR _Roland Fischer_

DATE _7/22/95_ TIME _1:15_

Dr. James Brown

OF _School of Int'l Business_

PHONE _617-443-3333_

FAX _617-442-4444_

MESSAGE: _Wrong diskettes were mailed. He is returning them. Please send new disks ASAP._

Please fax an answer to this claim. Apologize for the mistake. Tell him the new diskettes will go out by overnight mail.

New Tech Publications
454 Liberty Road
Philadelphia, PA 19145
TEL:215-652-8800 • FAX: 215-652-8181

New Tech
454 Liberty
Philadelphi
(215) 652-8

FAX COVER SHEE

DATE: July 27, 1995

TO: Dr. James Brown, De

CO.: School of Internat
Boston, MA

FROM: Roland Fischer, M

SUBJECT: Diskette Shipm

PAGES: this plus one

Dr. James Brown, Dean
School of International Business
540 Shawmut Avenue
Boston, MA 02118

Dear _____ _____:

Thank _____ for your telephone call of
_____ 22, 1995. We _____ for
the error in your _____.

To correct the error, the new diskettes will be sent
by _____ mail. You should _____
them tomorrow.

We are _____ for any _____

Sincerely,

Roland Fischer

Roland Fischer
Manager

Test Yourself

▶ *Read the following fax.*

F A X

W

WILSON & COMPANY, LTD.
51 Wimbleton Road
Toronto, Ontario M4D 2V8 • Canada
(416) 888-4444 • FAX:(416)999-4443

TO: Supplies Limited
FROM: Holly Park
DATE: June 5, 1994
REF: Purchase Order #0954-04
PAGES: 1
MESSAGE:

We received only five (5) cartons
of paper. We ordered fifty (50).
Please send them ASAP.

▶ *You work for Supplies Limited. Write an adjustment fax to Holly Park at Wilson & Company, Ltd.*

F • A • X

SUPPLIES LIMITED
Box 49
Oakville, Ontario L6J 7K1
Canada

GOOD BUSINESS NOTE

Sometimes the message in a fax is very short. This message can be typed on the cover sheet to save paper, time and money.

6A

Collection Letters

WORDS TO KNOW

balance
cancelled check
disregard
(to be) due
expiration
full payment
overdue
paid-in-full
partial payment
prompt
reminder
response

▶ *Read this conversation.*

Beth: The Higgins Company still hasn't paid its bill, Melissa.

Melissa: Still? Did you send a reminder, Beth?

Beth: Yes. About a month ago. Here it is.

FOLEY CONSTRUCTION
4590 Concord Avenue
Pittsburgh, Pennsylvania 15702
412-682-5671
FAX: 412-682-5671

December 4, 1994

Mary Stephens
Accountant
The Higgins Company
589 Curtis Road
Manassas, Virginia 22278

Ref: Account No. 4589-94

Dear Ms. Stephens:

The balance of $305.56 for invoice number 4589-94 was due on
November 1. This payment is now four weeks overdue. Our invoice
requests full payment in 30 days.

This is your second reminder. Please make full payment today.

We look forward to your prompt response.

Sincerely,

Beth Lynch
Credit Department

Beth:	Maybe I should send another reminder.
Melissa:	Yes, a stronger one this time!
Beth:	Okay. I'll even fax it!

▶ *Circle the correct answer.*

1. What is the problem?
   A. A reminder is due.   B. A payment is overdue.

2. What does Ms. Lynch want?
   A. Payment   B. References

3. Who wrote the collection letter?
   A. The Higgins Company   B. Foley Construction

4. What is a balance?
   A. The total amount due   B. A partial payment of the bill

5. Which word describes the letter?
   A. A reminder   B. A payment

6. Who works for the Higgins Company?
   A. Ms. Lynch   B. Ms. Stephens

7. Where does it say, "Full payment in 30 days."
   A. In the manual   B. On the invoice

balance	reminder
due	full payment
overdue	partial payment

▶ *Complete each sentence with a word from the box.*

1. The payment was _____ on November 1. Now it is overdue.

2. Ms. Lynch wants all of the invoice paid. She wants _____ of the bill.

3. Full payment is $305.56. If I make a partial payment of $100, the _____ is $205.56.

4. Full payment was due last month. Now, it is four weeks _____.

5. Beth Lynch sent a _____ to the company to pay its bill.

6. A payment of $100 would be _____ of the $305.56 bill.

MODEL FAX: Collection Letter

▶*Beth faxes a stronger collection letter. Read her fax.*

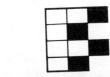

FOLEY CONSTRUCTION
4590 Concord Avenue
Pittsburgh, Pennsylvania 15702
412-682-5671
FAX: 412-682-5671

To: Mary Stephens   Tel: 703-555-3434
         The Higgins Company   Fax: 703-555-3435
         589 Curtis Road
         Manassas, VA 22278

From: Beth Lynch
         Credit Department

Date: January 8, 1995
Subject: Overdue Invoice
Ref: Account No.: 4589-94
Pages: This only

Message:
Your account balance of $305.56 is now two months
overdue.

As you know, payment was due on November 1, 1994.
Our invoice requests full payment in 30 days. We
have not received even partial payment. In fact,
we have not received any communication from you.

If we do not receive payment by January 10, we
will have to take appropriate action.

We look forward to your prompt response.

▶ *Circle the correct answer.*

1. Beth Lynch wrote this letter
   to get a job.
   A. Yes   B. No

2. This letter is a reminder to
   pay a bill.
   A. Yes   B. No

3. Ms. Stephens has sent partial
   payment.
   A. Yes   B. No

4. The payment is overdue.
   A. Yes   B. No

5. Ms. Lynch works for Foley
   Construction.
   A. Yes   B. No

6. The balance is $305.56.
   A. Yes   B. No

7. This fax is a little "stronger"
   than the December letter.
   A. Yes   B. No

COMMON BUSINESS EXPRESSIONS

Paid-in-Full   No money is owed.
Full Payment   No money is owed.
Partial Payment   Some money is owed.
Balance Due   Some or all money is owed.

BUSINESS STYLE: Body of a Collection Letter

The body of a collection letter generally has four parts.

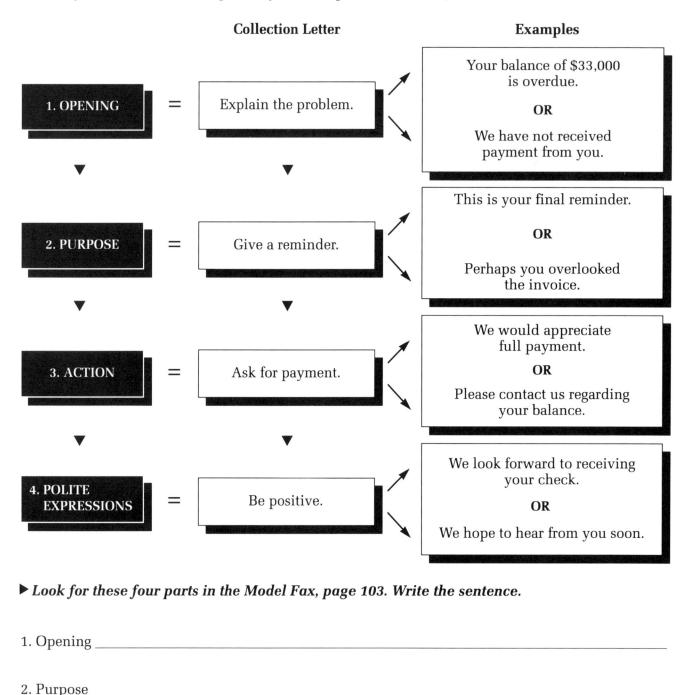

	Collection Letter		Examples
1. OPENING =	Explain the problem.		Your balance of $33,000 is overdue. **OR** We have not received payment from you.
2. PURPOSE =	Give a reminder.		This is your final reminder. **OR** Perhaps you overlooked the invoice.
3. ACTION =	Ask for payment.		We would appreciate full payment. **OR** Please contact us regarding your balance.
4. POLITE EXPRESSIONS =	Be positive.		We look forward to receiving your check. **OR** We hope to hear from you soon.

▶ *Look for these four parts in the Model Fax, page 103. Write the sentence.*

1. Opening _____

2. Purpose _____

3. Action _____

4. Polite Expressions _____

GRAMMAR: Run-on Sentences

A run-on sentence is a sentence that does not stop. It continues into the next sentence.

There are many ways of correcting run-on sentences. You can use punctuation (a semi-colon or a period), or you can use a clause marker.

Run-on:	Please remember to send your payment it is now overdue.
Corrected:	Please remember to send your payment; it is now overdue.
Corrected:	Please remember to send your payment. It is now overdue.
Corrected:	Please remember to send your payment since it is now overdue.

▶ *Circle the correct sentence.*

1. A.The invoice is due tomorrow, send the check today.

   B.The invoice is due tomorrow; send the check today.

2. A. Send a reminder to Mr. Simon, because his account is overdue.

   B. Send a reminder to Mr. Simon his account is overdue.

3. A. Please make full payment an envelope is enclosed.

   B. Please make full payment. An envelope is enclosed.

4. A. The invoice was due yesterday it was May 15.

   B. The invoice was due yesterday, May 15.

5. A. Your order will be shipped next Friday you should receive it by July 10.

   B. Your order will be shipped next Friday. You should receive it by July 10.

A sentence fragment is an incomplete sentence. See page 60 for review of *Sentence Fragments.*

▶ *Circle the correct answer.*

1. Because the shipment was damaged.	Fragment	Run-on
2. It weighs 25 pounds, the cost is extra.	Fragment	Run-on
3. When it is due.	Fragment	Run-on
4. You should prepare the purchase order fax the order.	Fragment	Run-on
5. Apologize to the customer, he's important.	Fragment	Run-on

Letter Practice 1

▶ *Correct the errors. Refer to the Model Fax on page 103.*

Type of Error	Number of Errors
Capitalization	5
Punctuation	4
No space	3
Omitted words	2
Repetitions	2
Letter order	2
Run-on sentence	1

RICHMOND'S DEPARTMENT STORE
696 Harbor Boulevard
Miami, Florida 32816
305-582-1660
FAX 305-582-7878

1 March 15, 1995

2 Lisa Vasquez
3 15 Johnson Street
4 Westfield, New Jersey 07090

5 Account No. 345-4503-454

6 Dear Ms. Vasquez:

7 The balance of $465.00 for invioce No. 780-82 due on may 15
8 This payment is is now six weeks overdue. our invoice
9 requests fullpayment in 30days

10 Please full payment today,

11 We lookforward to your prompt resopnse we have enclosed an
12 envelope for your convenience?

13 sincerely yours, ,

14 accounting department

Letter Practice 2

▶ *Use this information and the words from the box to complete the letter. Refer to the letter on page 101 for help.*

Albany	full	Sincerely
Avenue	Invoice	to
Corporation	look	yours
Dannon	May	
Dear	Mr.	

TO DO TODAY

Write - Tom Dannon of Amtel Corp.
Payment for Invoice #0980 due 5/26.
Full payment — $456.45
Tom Dannon
Amtel Corporation
458-43 Amsterdam Avenue
Albany, NY 11016

The
Top
Drawer

Greenwich, CT 06430
203-521-2383
FAX 203-521-2384

June 15, 1996

Tom Dannon

Amtel _____

458-43 Amsterdam _____

_____ , New York 11030

Reference: _____ #9080

_____ _____ _____:

The balance of _____ for the invoice reference above was due on _____ 26.

Please make _____ payment today.

We _____ forward _____ your prompt response.

_____ _____ ,

_____

Test Yourself

▶ *You work for Mr. Barn in the Collection Department. Read the following information and write a collection letter.*

FILLMORE INDUSTRIAL INC.
9854 EAST SPRINGFIELD DRIVE
SPRINGFIELD, IL 62705
217-927-9528
FAX 217-927-4002

From the desk of
James Barn, Collection Department

Write to Mrs. Claudia Spinosa, Accounting Department at Tire Manufacturing Company, 3490 Rydell Avenue, Dayton, OH 44012. Remind her that the payment for Invoice # 3498-49 was due 3 weeks ago. We want full payment— $569.66 .

MODEL LETTER: Reply to a Collection Letter

▶ *Read the following letter.*

The Higgins Company
589 Curtis Road
Manassas, Virginia 22278
703-555-3434
FAX 703-555-3435

January 3, 1995

Beth Lynch
Credit Department
Foley Construction
4590 Concord Avenue
Pittsburgh, Pennsylvania 15702

Dear Ms. Lynch:

We received your fax of January 3, 1995, today.

Your invoice 4589-94 dated October 1, 1993 was
paid-in-full on October 30, 1993. We are
enclosing a copy of the cancelled check which
was deposited by your company on November 5.

If you have any questions, please do not
hesitate to call.

Sincerely yours,

Mary Stephens

Mary Stephens
Accountant

▶ *Circle the correct answer.*

1. Who wrote the collection letter?
   A. Beth Lynch
   B. Mary Stephens

2. Who wrote the reply to the collection letter?
   A. Beth Lynch
   B. Mary Stephens

3. When did Mary receive the fax?
   A. January 3   B. January 4

4. When was the invoice sent?
   A. October 1   B. October 30

5. When was the invoice paid?
   A. October 1   B. October 30

6. Who deposited the check?
   A. Higgins Company
   B. Foley Construction

COMMON BUSINESS EXPRESSIONS

"Please do not hesitate..." is a very polite
expression.

Please do not hesitate to write.

Please do not hesitate to call.

Please do not hesitate to contact me.

BUSINESS STYLE: Body of a Reply to a Collection Letter

The body of a reply to a collection letter generally has four parts.

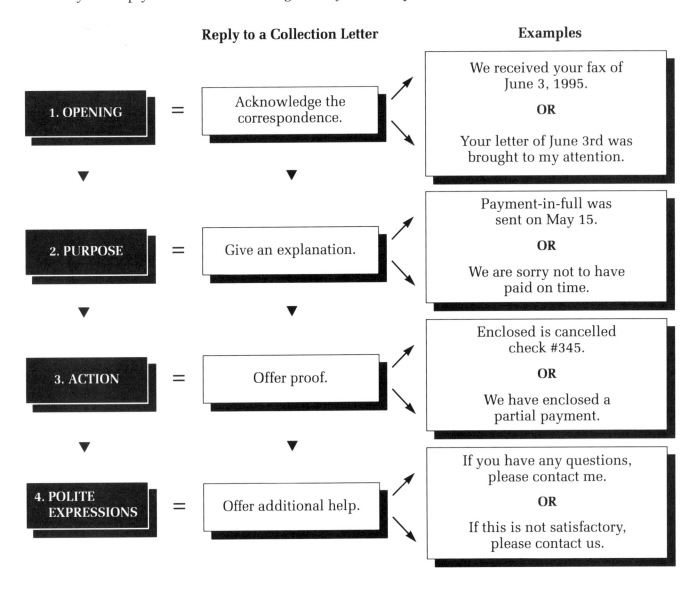

Reply to a Collection Letter **Examples**

1. OPENING = Acknowledge the correspondence.

We received your fax of June 3, 1995.

OR

Your letter of June 3rd was brought to my attention.

2. PURPOSE = Give an explanation.

Payment-in-full was sent on May 15.

OR

We are sorry not to have paid on time.

3. ACTION = Offer proof.

Enclosed is cancelled check #345.

OR

We have enclosed a partial payment.

4. POLITE EXPRESSIONS = Offer additional help.

If you have any questions, please contact me.

OR

If this is not satisfactory, please contact us.

▶ *Look for these four parts in the Model Letter, page 109. Write the sentences.*

1. Opening _____

2. Purpose _____

3. Action _____

4. Polite Expressions _____

GRAMMAR: Negative Words

Negative words express the idea of no:

not	never
no one	nobody
nothing	none
hardly	scarcely
neither	nor
neither...nor	rarely

Use only one negative expression in a sentence:
Mr. Frette did not ask anyone for help.
(not "no one")

Correct
Mr. Frette did not ask anyone for help.
Mr. Frette asked no one for help.

Incorrect
Mr. Frette did not ask no one for help.

▶ *Circle the correct answer.*

1. Some customers do not (ever/never) make full payments.

2. Ms. Jones has not done (nothing/anything) about the overdue payment.

3. They hardly (never/ever) pay on time.

4. The secretary never (does not fill/fills) out the forms correctly.

5. Neither Keiko (or/nor) Masako knew the address.

6. My secretary rarely (ever/never) make typos.

7. He did not ask for (nobody/anybody).

8. Janice never needs help with (anything/nothing).

9. I cannot find (no/any) paper clips.

10. Neither Mrs. Simon (or/nor) her secretary returned my call.

Letter Practice 1

▶ *Use this information to write a reply to the collection letter below. Refer to the Model Letter on page 109.*

FROM THE DESK OF
Roger Light, *Manager*

Tell her we paid in full on August 10 — send her a copy of check # 4253 which was deposited August 14.

METROPOLITAN
Credit Company
7698 Westside Highway
Chicago, IL 60652
312-663-5823
FAX 312-663-1223

September 15, 1994

Mr. Roger Light
City Books
131 Townsend Street
San Francisco, California 94107

Dear Mr. Light:

The balance of $3,543.00 for invoice No. 321 was due on August 15.
This payment is now two weeks overdue.

Please make full payment immediately.

We look forward to your prompt response.

Sincerely yours,

Sarah Good

Sarah Good
Accounting Department

SG/mm

City Books
131 Townsend Street
San Francisco, CA 94107
415-962-5577
FAX 415-962-8956

September 20, 1994

Sarah Good

_____ Department

Metropolitan Credit Company

7698 Westside Highway

_____ , Illinois 60652

Dear Ms. Good:

We _____ your letter of _____ 15, 1994.

Your _____ No.321 dated August 1, 1994 was paid in

_____ on _____ 10.   I am enclosing a

copy of the cancelled check which was deposited by your company on

_____ 14.

If you have _____ questions, please do

_____ hesitate to _____ .

Sincerely yours,

Roger Light

Roger Light

Manager

RL/_____

Fax Practice 1

▶ *Respond to this collection letter by fax.*

Atlas Insurance
45 Southeast Parkway
Los Angeles, California 92187
Tel: 916-564-5000
Fax: 916-564-5100

May 6, 1994

Ms. Angela Woo
President
Prometheus Ironworks, Inc.
2nd Floor, No. 952
Tun Hwa, North Road
Taipei, Taiwan

Ref: ID# 483754291
           Insurance Coverage Expires: 05/31/94

Dear Ms. Woo:

According to our records, we have not received your payment for
the month of May, 1994. If you have recently made this payment,
please disregard this letter. If you have not, please send a
copy of this letter together with a payment of fifty U.S.
dollars (US$50.00).

Please send your payment before May 31, 1994, or your insurance
will be cancelled.

We look forward to hearing from you soon.

Sincerely,

John Worth
Claims Department

▶ *Use this information to prepare your reply.*

from the desk of
ANGELA WOO

Paid #50 on April 15, 1994
Check # 425 enclosed
Deposited by Atlas Insurance
on April 19

**PROMETHEUS
IRONWORKS, INC.**
2nd Floor, No. 952
Tun Hwa, North Road
Taipei, Taiwan
886-623-5681
FAX 886-623-8723

FAX TRANSMISSION

TO: _____
       _____
       _____
       _____

FAX: _____   **TEL:** _____

FROM: Angela Woo, President

DATE: _____   **PAGES:** _____

REF: Your Fax of June 6, 1994
        Expiration of Insurance Policy: ID # 483754291

MESSAGE:

We _____ your letter of _____ 6, 1994.

Payment for the month of _____ was paid in _____ on
_____ 15.   I am enclosing a copy of the cancelled check no.
_____ which was deposited by your company on _____
19_____ .

If you have _____ questions, please do _____
hesitate to _____ .

Sincerely yours,

Angela Woo

Angela Woo
President

Test Yourself

▶ *Read the following information and reply to the letter.*
Refer to the Model Letter on page 109 for help.

From the Desk of: James Shinsky

Please answer this letter.
We paid in full on June 16.
Copy the cancelled check
no. 3557 and send it to
them.

Benson's Supplies
45 Griffith Road
Dinsdale, Hamilton
North Island, New Zealand
17-521-4628
FAX 17-521-8383

July 30, 1994

James Shinsky
Plumbing Associates
674 Groger Street
South Island, New Zealand

Dear Mr. Shinsky:

We have not received your June payment for $103.50
for Invoice #592. It is now four weeks overdue.

Please send it to us today in the enclosed envelope.

We look forward to your prompt response.

The Credit Department
Benson's Supplies

Plumbing Associates
674 Groger Street
South Island, New Zealand

FINAL TEST: Grammar, Punctuation, Format, and Style

▶ **A. Label the parts of this letter.**
  B. What is the format of this letter: block, semi-block, or indented?
  C. Correct the errors. Rewrite the letter.

Type of Error	Number of Errors
Style: Formal/Informal	4
Capitalization	9
Punctuation	8
Letter order	3
Word order	1
Repetition	1
Negative word	1
Run-on sentence	1
Sentence fragment	1
Letter format	3
Grammar	1

International **Graphics**
1075 California Street
Chicago, Illinois 60613
(312) 775-9696 fax: (312) 775-4934

1 ms. Eleanor Chazam
2 manager, Bookstore
3 Sanno gallery of Art
4 32 Crestwood Avenue
5 may 21 1996
6 Houston texas 77007

7 Ms. Dear Chazam,

8 thank you for your letter of may 15, 1996 I'm sorry to hear
9 hear that the carton of books were damaged

10   Our comapnys policy is to replace damaged books.   I
11 want you to accept the replacement without charge. I'll ask
12 Mr. Robert smith, Accounting Assistant, to not send the
13 invoice for the books

14 I'll sned the books by overnight mail. Call when they
15 arrive?

16 Again, I regret the inconvenience but no one from our
17 department was not aware the carton was damaged.

18 Look forwrad to serving you in the future?

19 *Mark Chang*
20 Mark Chang
21 shipping Department

International **Graphics**
1075 California Street
Chicago, Illinois 60613
(312) 775-9696 fax: (312) 775-4934

Reference

Letters

FORMAT

The format of your correspondence is determined by office policy. The format depends on where you place your margins and how you type the letter.

A margin is the blank space that frames a letter. There are four margins in a letter. The width of the margins will depend on your office stationery and office style.

There are three formats for business correspondence: block, semi-block; and indented.

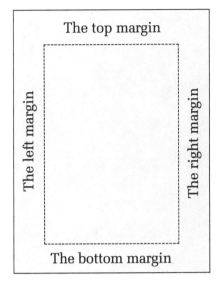

The top margin

The left margin

The right margin

The bottom margin

Block

This letter is written in block style. Everything begins at the left margin — flush left.

MSG Systems Inc.
1781 Orange Blossom Lane • Suite 509
Orlando Florida 32817
(407) 232-0880   Fax (407) 476-0455

December 3, 1995

Rosa Tucci
General Television Services
1600 East Grand Avenue
Chicago, Illinois 60611

Dear Ms. Tucci:

Thank you for your inquiry about our telephone answering machines and voice mail systems. I am enclosing brochures on our products.

A sales representative will be in Orlando next week. We will call you to schedule an appointment.

Again, thank you for your interest.

Sincerely yours,

Hazan Ozal
Marketing Manager

cc: V. Alfonso, Sales Representative

Semi-Block

This letter is written in semi-block style. Everything begins at the left margin — except for the date and closing.

Wilson New Media
P.O. Box 12456
Chaswick, Pennsylvania 15024
(412) 274-8490 • Fax (412) 274-6652

August 16, 1994

Industrial Training Center
University of Exeter
Exeter, Devon, England EX1 2LU

Dear Sir or Madam:

We read about you training programs in the Training Gazette of June, 1994. We train workers in industry in this country and are always looking for new materials.

We would appreciate receiving information on your Center and your materials.

We look forward to hearing from you at your earliest convenience.

Sincerely yours,

Ralston Crawl
Program Manager

Indented

This letter is written in the indented style. Every paragraph is indented.

Ferranti Management Consulting Associates
730 Key Parkway, Suite 935
Westwood, Massachusetts 02090
(617) 325-8522 • Fax (617) 325-9412

August 16, 1994

Complete Video
950 Northside Drive
Nashville, Tennessee 37203

Dear Sir or Madam:

    On May 15, we ordered six (6) color television monitors. You sent sixty (60).

    We are returning fifty-four (54) monitors to you today. Please correct the invoice.

Sincerely yours,

Tom Grayson
Purchasing Manager

EXERCISE 1: FORMAT

▶ *Rewrite these letters on your own paper.*

1. Rewrite the Block format letter on page 121 in Semi-block format.
2. Rewrite the Semi-block format letter on page 122 in Indented format.
3. Rewrite the Indented format letter above in Block format.
4. Rewrite the Block format letter on page 121 in Indented format.
5. Rewrite the Semi-block format letter on page 122 in Block format.
6. Rewrite the Indented format letter above in Semi-block format.

PARTS OF A LETTER

These are the parts of a letter.

```
                                              ┌─────────────────┐
                                              │ Return Address  │
                                              └─────────────────┘

        ┌──────────────────┐
        │ Date             │
        └──────────────────┘
        ┌──────────────────┐
        │ Inside Address   │
        └──────────────────┘
        ┌──────────────────────┐
        │ Greeting or Salutation│
        └──────────────────────┘
        ┌────────────────────────────────────────┐
        │ Body                                    │
        │                                         │
        │                                         │
        │                                         │
        └────────────────────────────────────────┘

        ┌──────────────────┐
        │ Closing          │
        └──────────────────┘
        ┌──────────────────┐
        │ Signature        │
        └──────────────────┘
        ┌──────────────────┐
        │ Typed Name       │
        └──────────────────┘
        ┌──────────────────┐
        │ Enclosure        │
        └──────────────────┘
        ┌──────────┐
        │ cc:      │
        └──────────┘
```

EXERCISE 2: PARTS OF A LETTER

▶ *Label the parts of the letter.*

```
                                    _____ 16 North Road
                                                Berkeley, California 95436

                                    _____ June 29, 1993

    Mrs. R. E. Bok
    Human Resources Director
    Perle Employment Agency _____
    1900 Grant Avenue
    San Francisco, California 92654

    Dear Mrs. Bok: _____

        I am applying for the position of secretary
    which was advertised in the San Francisco Chronicle
    of June 28.
                                                          _____
        I have enclosed my resume, and I would like to
    schedule an interview. I will call you early next week.

        I look forward to discussing this position with you.

                                    Sincerely yours, _____

                                    Annette Lee      _____
                                    Annette Lee      _____
```

Return Address

The Return Address contains:

Your street address	1818 H Street
Your city, state, and ZIP Code	Washington, DC 20433

A comma separates the city from the state or country.

Example:

Berkeley, California	Madrid, Spain
City, State	**City, Country**

A comma separates the state or province from the country.

Example:

Toronto, Ontario, Canada
City, Province, Country

EXERCISE 3: RETURN ADDRESS

▶ *Cross out the line that does NOT belong in the return address.*

Example:

A. 44 Belmont Road

B. Armonk, New York 10504

~~C. Enclosure~~

1. A. 806 Connecticut Avenue
   B. Dear Mr. Brown
   C. Washington, D.C.

2. A. Sincerely yours,
   B. 316 Anderson Road
   C. Coral Gables, Florida 33134

3. A. 680 Vine Street
   B. Seattle, Washington 02149
   C. May 16,1994

4. A. cc: Dr. Ralph Carson
   B. 55 Chapel Street
   C. Newton, Massachusetts 02160

EXERCISE 4: RETURN ADDRESS

▶ *Put a comma in the addresses below.*

Example:
New York City **,** New York

1. Milwaukee Wisconsin

2. Paris France

3. Seoul Korea

4. Brisbane Queensland Australia

5. Chicago Illinois

6. Montreal Quebec Canada

7. Dallas Texas

8. Mexico City DF Mexico

Date

The date of a letter can be put in several places in the letter. The date is usually (1) under the return address or (2) at the left margin. Some writers put the date (3) under the typed name at the bottom of the letter or (4) in the middle under the company address on the letterhead stationery.

Dates are not abbreviated in business letters. A comma separates the month and day from the year.

In international correspondence dates can be confusing if only numbers are used. You must sometimes clarify the date.

American Form:	month/day/year	Alternate Form:	day/month/year
	January 12, 1995		12 January, 1995

EXERCISE 5: DATE

▶ *Complete the chart.*

Number	Month	Abbreviation	Number	Month	Abbreviation
1	January	Jan.	7	July	July
2	February	Feb.	8	_____	Aug.
3	_____	Mar.	9	_____	Sept.
4	_____	Apr.	10	_____	Oct.
5	_____	May	11	_____	Nov.
6	June	June	12	December	Dec.

EXERCISE 6: DATE

▶ *Rewrite the following dates.*

Example:
6.17.94   June 17, 1994 _____

1. 7/15/92   _____   3. 7-18-93   _____

2. Feb. 9, 1993   _____   4. Oct. 5, '92   _____

EXERCISE 7: DATE

▶ *Rewrite the following dates to clarify the correct date.*

Example:
1/6/90   Do you mean January 6, 1990 or June 1, 1990 ? _____

1. 8/12/95   _____

2. 7/5/96   _____

3. 11/4/97   _____

4. 3/10/94   _____

5. 9/2/95   _____

Inside Address

The inside address contains:

The Addressee's Title, First Name, Last Name	Mr. Bill Rubin
Job Title	Vice President of Operations
Company Name	Garnet Educational Services
Street Address	1525 Dexter Avenue, Suite 200
City, State, ZIP Code	Seattle, Washington 98109

In the United States, the house or building number comes before the street. In some countries, the number comes after the street.

Examples:

Jan Hoisus
Manager, Public Relations Department
European Discs, Ltd.
Leliegracht, 46
Amsterdam 1015 DH
Netherlands

Dr. S. Lukenbill
Director, Sales and Marketing
Data Computers
Bonnesfontaines, 18
1700 Fribourg
Switzerland

EXERCISE 8: INSIDE ADDRESS

▶ *These are addresses in the United States. Write them in the correct order.*

Example:
Ward Circle 52   52 Ward Circle

1. Adams Street 65 _____

2. Street Jones 21 _____

3. Rowe Avenue 145 _____

4. Fifth Avenue 104 _____

Greeting

The Greeting should use the reader's name if known.

When you know the reader's name:

Dear + (title) + Last Name: Dear Mr. Maxwell:

When you do NOT know the reader's name:

Use Sir or Madam: Dear Sir or Madam

EXERCISE 9: GREETING

▶ *Circle the correct greeting.*

Example:

A. Dear:
B. Dear Ms. Pool: *(circled)*

1. A. Dear Mr. West:
   B. Mr. Dear West:

2. A. Dear Rex Reid:
   B. Dear Mr. Reid:

3. A. Dear Mrs.:
   B. Dear Mrs. Tyne:

4. A. Dear Bier Dr.:
   B. Dear Dr. Bier:

▶ *Write these greetings correctly.*

Example:
Mrs. Dear Gordon: Dear Mrs. Gordon

5. Mr. Dear Komai: _____

6. Dear Locke Dr.: _____

7. Dear Ms. Press _____

8. Ms. Dear Burne: _____

Body

The body of a letter tells why you are writing. There are generally four parts to the body of a letter:

Opening:	Give your reason for writing.
Purpose:	Provide the details of why you are writing.
Action:	Tell what will happen next.
Polite Expression:	Thank the reader.

Closing

There are two types of closing — formal and informal.

Formal: If you do not know the person's name or if you use the person's last name in the greeting, you may use either the formal or the standard closing.

Informal: If you use the person's first name in the greeting, you may use the informal closing.

Formal		**Standard**		**Informal**	
Greeting	*Closing*	*Greeting*	*Closing*	*Greeting*	*Closing*
Dear Sir or Madam:	Yours very truly,	Dear Mr. Smith:	Sincerely,	Dear Joe,	Sincerely,
	Very truly yours,		Yours sincerely,		Sincerely yours,
	Very sincerely yours,		Cordially yours,		Cordially,
	Very cordially yours,				Yours truly,
	Sincerely yours,				

EXERCISE 10: CLOSING

▶ *Write the closings for letters with the following greetings.*

Example:

Dear Mr. Gant: ___Sincerely yours,___

Greeting   Closing

1. Dear Mrs. Wilcox: _____

2. Dear Mary, _____

3. Dear Sir or Madam: _____

4. Dear Mr. White and Mr. Wong: _____

Signature/Typed Name

The writer of the letter will have his or her name typed at the bottom of the letter with his or her title. This person will then sign the letter.

In some offices, a secretary will put his or her initials at the bottom of the letter. This shows who typed the letter. The writer's initials come first, and they are capitalized. The typist's initials come next, and they are not capitalized.

> JP/rs
> Writer/typist

cc's

The letters *cc* stand for *carbon copy*, which is how copies were first made before photocopiers and computer printers. Today a "cc:" tells us who else received a copy of the letter.

Note: cc is not capitalized.

FOLDING A LETTER

When a reader opens your letter, the first thing he or she must see is the letterhead and date; the second thing is the body of the letter, and finally, the signature.

Fold a letter like this:

Draw 2 lines (with your eye — not with a pencil) to divide the letter into three equal parts.

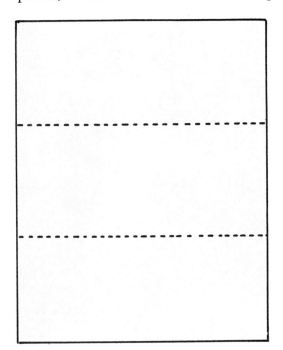

Fold the bottom of the letter to the top line.

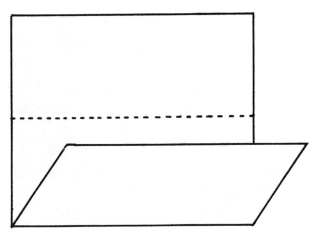

Fold the top third of the letter over.

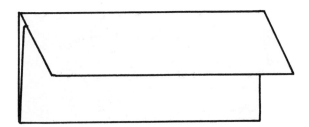

GOOD BUSINESS NOTE
When a letter is taken from the envelope, it should be seen the way it is to be read.

Envelopes

FORMAT

Most companies have envelopes with their companies' name printed on them. A secretary will only type the mailing address and stamp the letter.

PARTS OF AN ENVELOPE

(Return Address)

First Name (or Initial) • Last Name
Building/House number • Street
City, State • ZIP Code

(Return Address)

Title • First Name (or Initial) • Last Name
Job Title
Company Name
Street number • Street name
City, State • ZIP Code

EXERCISE 11: PARTS OF AN ENVELOPE

▶ *Look at this envelope.*

New Jersey Power Company
5695 South 23rd Road
Ridgefield, NJ 08887

Mr. Frederick Wolf
Director of Marketing
Smith Printing Company
590 Sixth Avenue
Milwaukee, WI 53216

▶ *Circle the correct answer.*

1. What is the ZIP Code in the return address?
   A. 08887   B. 53216

2. What is the ZIP Code in the mailing address?
   A. 08887   B. 53216

3. What is WI?
   A. Wisconsin   B. West Indies

4. What state does the letter come from?
   A. WI   B. NJ

5. What state will the letter go to?
   A. WI   B. NJ

Memos

FORMAT

A memo is generally correspondence written from one person in a company to another in the same company. The format is usually a block format.

PARTS OF A MEMO

A memo has five parts:

| TO: | John Quinn

There is no need for an address if the memo goes to workers in the same company. Titles like Mr. and Mrs. are generally not used in a Memo Address.

| FROM: | Maria Landry *ML*

Instead of a signature, the sender signs his or her initials. Work titles like Manager are optional. They may or may not be used.

| DATE: | January 4, 1993

The date in a memo is usually written on the left side.

| SUBJECT: | Company Health Insurance Policy

The subject line is sometimes abbreviated as "SUB:." The subject line tells what the memo is about.

| BODY: |

The body of a memo discusses the subject.

EXERCISE 12: PARTS OF A MEMO

▶ *Draw a line between the matching parts.*

Example

TO: — May 16, 1994

FROM: — M. Goldwyn

DATE: — Office Furniture

SUBJECT: — S. Rattner *SR*

1.

TO: — M. Forbet *MF*

FROM: — Health Care

DATE: — R. Winston

SUBJECT: — December 15, 1994

2.

TO: — Travel Insurance

FROM: — August 8, 1995

DATE: — S. Royce *SR*

SUB: — G. Seward

3.

TO: — March 19, 1993

FROM: — Part-time Employees

DATE: — M. Crowl

SUBJ: — S. Marko *SM*

4.

TO: — R. Thompson

FROM: — Employee Benefits

DATE: — Pete Williams *PW*

SUBJECT: — June 17, 1996

Electronic Mail

FORMAT

Many companies send interoffice messages through the computer. Messages sent by computer are called Electronic Mail or E-Mail.

A company can link all of its employees in one office by a computer or it can link its employees in offices around the country by a computer.

PARTS OF ELECTRONIC MAIL

There are usually six parts to an E-mail transmission. Look at this example.

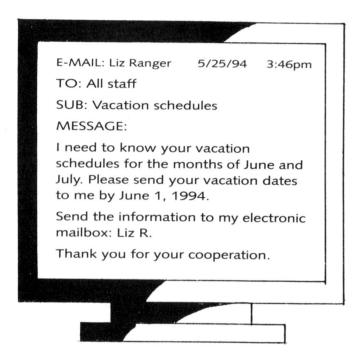

E-MAIL: Liz Ranger   5/25/94   3:46pm

TO: All staff

SUB: Vacation schedules

MESSAGE:

I need to know your vacation schedules for the months of June and July. Please send your vacation dates to me by June 1, 1994.

Send the information to my electronic mailbox: Liz R.

Thank you for your cooperation.

The sender's name, date and the time are usually supplied by the computer. You only type in the name of the person receiving the message, the subject and the message.

EXERCISE 13: PARTS OF ELECTRONIC MAIL

▶ *Circle the correct answer. Use the E-mail transmission above.*

1. Who wrote the memo?

    A. The staff   B. Liz Ranger

2. Who got the memo?

    A. The staff   B. Liz Ranger

3. What is the memo about?

    A. Liz's vacation   B. The staff's vacation dates

4. When should the staff send the information?

    A. In June and July   B. Before June 1

5. How should the staff reply?

    A. By electronic mail   B. In person

Faxes

FORMAT

A fax (or facsimile) is a piece of correspondence sent over the phone lines. A long fax is more expensive to send than a short one. Be concise.

Most businesses have a separate telephone line just for the fax. This is called a dedicated line. The telephone line is dedicated to the fax. When a fax has its own line, faxes can be received and sent 24 hours a day.

PARTS OF A FAX

A fax transmission often has two parts:

A Cover Sheet

If the first page has attachments, then the first page is called a cover sheet or cover page.

Attachments

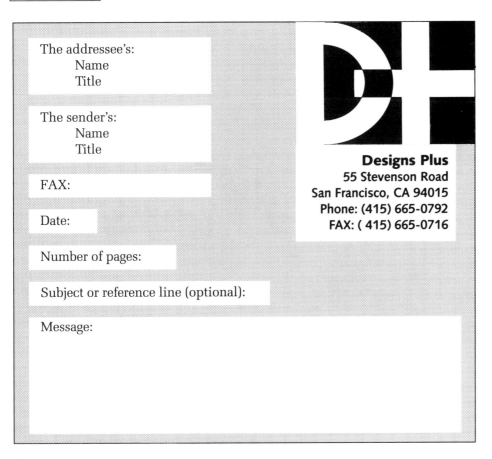

The addressee's:
    Name
    Title

The sender's:
    Name
    Title

FAX:

Date:

Number of pages:

Subject or reference line (optional):

Message:

Designs Plus
55 Stevenson Road
San Francisco, CA 94015
Phone: (415) 665-0792
FAX: (415) 665-0716

Pages

It is important to tell how many pages are included. One or more pages may be lost during transmission. This is done in several ways.

```
Pages: This + 2     (total 3 pages)
Pages: Cover + 4    (total 5 pages)
Pages: This only    (total 1 pages)
Pages: 5            (total 5 pages)
```

It is important to have phone numbers. If a page is missing, you can call and ask the sender to transmit the fax again.

EXERCISE 14: PARTS OF A FAX

▶ *Write the total number of pages in each fax.*

Example		Total Pages
Pages:	This + 7	**8**
1. Pages:	This plus 1	_____
2. Pages:	Cover only	_____
3. Pages:	Cover + 3	_____
4. Pages:	This + 5	_____
5. Pages:	6	_____

EXERCISE 15: PARTS OF A FAX

▶ *Find and correct the errors below.*

Types of Errors	Number of Errors
Punctuation	3
Capitalization	11
Pronouns	3
Style: Formal/Informal	1

---

1 **FAX TRANSMISSION**

damen printers, inc.
101 Gould Street
Wakefield, MA 01880
(617) 246-0200

2 Date: january 16, 1994

3 To: reservations Manager

4   ritz hotel, paris. france

5 TEL: 01-33-1-42-60-38-30

6 FAX: 01-33-1-42-60-23-71

7 From: james grant,

8   manager

9 pages: this

10 Subject: Reservation Confirmation

11 As we discussed in us telephone conversation this morning. I want to confirm my

12 hotel reservation for two (2) nights. I will arrive on August 11. I will leave on

13 August 13.

14 I will be arriving on French Airways at 11:39 p.m. from New York.

15 Please guarantee my reservation with me American Travel card, number 325444-43156-

16 78, expiration date 4/94.

17 I look forward to my stay at you hotel,

Common Abbreviations

ABBREVIATION PUNCTUATION
A period always follows an initial.

Thomas Lee Preston   T.L. Preston
Margaret Simpson Bates   Margaret S. Bates

A period generally follows an abbreviation.

page	p.
Company	Co.
Corporation	Corp.
Street	St.
Doctor	Dr.
Mister	Mr.
number	no.
international	int'l.
Limited	Ltd.
Incorporated	Inc.

There are some abbreviations that do NOT use periods:

Eastern Standard Time	EST
as soon as possible	ASAP
very important person	VIP
close of business	COB
Personal Computer	PC
Vice President	VP
Date of Birth	DOB

Some abbreviations use slashes:

05/16/76	May 16, 1976
08/25	August 25
c/o	in care of
D/d	delivered
O/S	out of stock
N/A	not applicable

EXERCISE 16: ABBREVIATIONS
▶ *Write the correct abbreviations.*

7/2/50	EST	c/o	DOB	NYA	ASAP	D/d	O/S	VIP

1. 10:00 Eastern Standard Time   10:00 _____

2. July 2, 1950   _____

3. Date of Birth   _____

4. New York, New York   New York, _____

5. In care of Dr. Gibbons   _____ Dr. Gibbons

6. Out of stock item No. 3454; will back order   _____ item No. 3454; will back order

7. Delivered on Sept. 24, 1994   _____ on Sept 24, 1994

8. Please send the memo as soon as possible!   Please send the memo _____

9. Invite Janet. She's a very important person!   Invite Janet. She's a _____

EXERCISE 17: ABBREVIATIONS
▶ *Write the abbreviation of the underlined word. Add periods where necessary.*

Example:

Mister P T Vitale   Mr. P.T. Vitale

1. Item <u>number</u>   _____

2. Mutual Insurance <u>Company</u>   _____

3. South <u>Street</u>   _____

4. <u>Doctor</u> R E Brown   _____

5. (Your Initials and Last Name)   _____

STATES

Alabama	AL	Kentucky	KY		
Alaska	AK	Louisiana	LA	Oklahoma	OK
American Samoa	AS	Maine	ME	Oregon	OR
Arizona	AZ	Maryland	MD	Pennsylvania	PA
Arkansas	AR	Massachusetts	MA	Puerto Rico	PR
California	CA	Michigan	MI	Rhode Island	RI
Canal Zone	CZ	Minnesota	MN	South Carolina	SC
Colorado	CO	Mississippi	MS	South Dakota	SD
Connecticut	CT	Missouri	MO	Tennessee	TN
Delaware	DE	Montana	MT	Texas	TX
District of Columbia	DC	Nebraska	NE	Trust Territories	TT
Florida	FL	Nevada	NV	Utah	UT
Georgia	GA	New Hampshire	NH	Vermont	VT
Guam	GU	New Jersey	NJ	Virginia	VA
Hawaii	HI	New Mexico	NM	Virgin Islands	VI
Idaho	ID	New York	NY	Washington	WA
Illinois	IL	North Carolina	NC	West Virginia	WV
Indiana	IN	North Dakota	ND	Wisconsin	WI
Iowa	IA	Northern Mariana Is.	CM	Wyoming	WY
Kansas	KS	Ohio	OH		

TYPES OF STREETS

Here are the names of types of streets and their abbreviations. You may use abbreviations on envelopes, but you should not use abbreviations in the letter.

Street	St.	Avenue	Ave.
Boulevard	Blvd.	Lane	Ln.
Road	Rd.	Highway	Hwy.
Drive	Dr.		

MONETARY UNITS

Country	Monetary Unit	Abbreviation	Country	Monetary Unit	Abbreviation
Australia	dollar	$A	Mexico	peso	$
Austria	schilling	S	New Zealand	dollar	$NZ
Canada	dollar	Can$	Poland	zloty	zl.
Czechoslovakia	korona	Kcs	Singapore	dollar	$
France	franc	Fr	Spain	peseta	Pta/Pts
Germany	deutsch mark	DM	South Korea	won	W
Greece	drachma	Dr	Switzerland	franc	SwF
Hong Kong	dollar	$HK	Taiwan	dollar/yuan	N.T. $
Italy	lira	L	United Kingdom	pound	£
Japan	yen	¥	United States	dollar	$US

EXERCISE 18: ABBREVIATIONS

▶ *Match the appropriate abbreviation with the correct country.*

_____ 1. Pta A. Switzerland

_____ 2. DM B. Greece

_____ 3. ¥ C. United Kingdom

_____ 4. SwF D. Korea

_____ 5. £ E. Spain

_____ 6. Dr F. Germany

_____ 7. won G. Japan

_____ 8. S H. Austria

Reading Aloud

SLASH

1. Slash means "for each" when a number comes before it. $29.95/carton means "The price is $29.95 for each carton."

$22.45/dozen	$22.45 per dozen or $22.45 for a dozen
$13.66/gross	$13.66 per gross or $13.66 for a gross
$1.95/box	$1.95 per box or $1.95 for a box
$9.88/2	$9.88 for two

Note: You do NOT read "per" when a number follows the slash (/).

2. Slash (/) means "and" when it separates two nouns.

Shipping/Handling is the cost to prepare, pack, and send an order. It is usually a percentage of the total cost of the order.

ASAP

ASAP = as soon as possible

You can read this out loud and say only the letters "A-S-A-P" or you can say "as soon a possible."

EXT

Ext. = telephone extension number

You can read EXT out loud as "extension."

X

8½″ x 11″ = 8½ inches wide by 11 inches tall.

You can read x as "by."

Answer Key

TEST YOURSELF

Page 7
Errors in lines:
1. August 15, 1994
2. Mr.; M.; Ramirez
4. Soup
6. Angeles
7. Dear Mr. Ramirez
8. Your; morning
9. Please tell; plans, (comma); we will; airport. (period)
10. company
11. month. (period)
12. Sincerely; yours, (comma)
14. Bill

UNIT 1A

Page 9
1. Human Resources Director
2. secretary
3. job
4. apply
5. advertisement

Page 10
Students circle:
1. B. Annette Lee
2. A. Mrs. Bok
3. B. 16 North Road
4. B. Her resumé
5. A. Human Resources Director
6. B. June 29

Page 11
1. I am applying for the position of secretary which was advertised in the San Francisco Chronicle of June 28.
2. I have enclosed my resume, and I would like to schedule an interview.
3. I will call you early next week.
4. I look forward to discussing this position with you.

Page 12
1. Dear James,
2. Dear Mrs. Smith:
3. Dear Dr. Marker:
4. Dear Mr. Tenley:
5. Dear Susan,
6. Dear Ms. Lee:
7. Dear Martha,

Page 13
1. were
2. was
3. wants
4. want
5. writes
6. write
7. has
8. have
9. is
10. are

Page 14
1. I would like a new job.
2. I would like an interview.
3. I would like to apply for the position.
4. I would like to enclose my resumé.
5. I would like to call you soon.
6. I would like to change jobs.

Page 15
1. Milwaukee, Wisconsin
2. 590 Sixth Avenue
3. Dear Mr. Wolf:
4. am
5. position
6. secretary
7. was
8. have
9. would like
10. Sincerely

Page 16
Mr.; East; Street; Mr.; am; position; July; Monthly; my; like; week; yours

Page 17
1. Times
2. 9
3. Receptionist
4. Goodman; Communications; Avenue; CA

LETTERS WILL VARY BUT MUST CLOSELY FOLLOW FORMAT PRESENTED IN PART A MODEL LETTER.

UNIT 1B

Page 18
Students circle:
1. A. yes
2. A. yes
3. A. yes
4. B. no
5. B. no
6. A. yes

Page 19
1. Thank you for sending your letter and resumé.
2. We appreciate your interest in the Perle Employment Agency.
3. We would like to schedule an interview on Monday, July 8 at 9 a.m.
4. We look forward to talking with you.

Page 20
1. July; E
2. Dear Mary; F
3. International Systems Co.; D
4. There are many applicants.; A
5. Chicago; B
6. Sincerely; G
7. Thanksgiving; E
8. Monday; E

9. Dr. Winslow; C
10. Los Angeles, California; B

Page 21
Corrections in lines:
1. February
2. Mr. Andrew Pan
3. 63 Fifth Street
4. Melbourne, 2085 Victoria
5. Australia
6. Dear Mr. Pan
7. Thank; They
8. February
9. We; Gift Galleries
10. Wednesday
11. Please
12. We
13. Sincerely

Page 22
1. of
2. at
3. on
4. at
5. on
6. on

Page 23
Corrections in lines:
4. Tokyo; Japan
5. Dear Mr. Hiratsuma (3)
7. on; September
8. We
9. on; Tuesday; at
10. Please
12. Sincerely

Page 24
Mr.; Reilly; letter; resumé; on; Shop-A-Lot; like; on; yours

Page 25
LETTERS WILL VARY BUT MUST CLOSELY FOLLOW FORMAT PRESENTED IN PART B MODEL LETTER.

UNIT 2A

Page 27
1. planner
2. attend
3. meeting
4. planning
5. confirm

Page 28
Students circle:
1. A. Curt Marks
2. B. Jan Turner
3. B. Baltimore, MD
4. B. A TV and VCR
5. A. Three

Page 29
1. In our telephone conversation yesterday, we discussed plans for our meeting at your conference center.

2. I have additional requests: *etc.*
3. I would appreciate your answers by next Friday.
4a. If you need anymore information please call me.
4b. I would like to thank you for your help in planning our meeting.

Page 30
Students circle:
1. B. No, I don't.
2. A. Yes, I did.
3. B. No, she hasn't.
4. B. Yes, they will.
5. A. Yes, it has.
6. B. Yes, I did.
7. A. No, I couldn't.
8. A. Yes, he will.

Students circle:
1. B. No, it isn't.
2. A. An hour ago.
3. B. Yes, you may.
4. B. Yes, it will.
5. A. A VCR

Page 31
1. What
2. How long
3. When
4. Where
5. How many

1. B. No, it isn't.
2. A. An hour ago.
3. B. Yes, you may.
4. B. Yes, it will.
5. A. A VCR.
6. A. Yes, I do.

Page 32
Corrections in lines:
8. . (period)
10. . (period)
11. ? (question mark)
12. ? (question mark)
13. ? (question mark)
14. ? (question mark)
15. ? (question mark)
16. ? (question mark)
17. . (period)

Page 33
Company: Cellular Phone Company·
Meeting Location: Arrowhead Conference Center
Arrival Date, Day, Time: March 15
Departure Date, Day, Time: March 17
Number of people attending: 51-100
Rooms Required: 2
Audiovisual Requirements:
TV/VCR
Seating:
Tables: 20
Catering:
Lunch - March 16
Contact:
Name: Curt Marks
Dept: Special Projects Office
Telephone: 301-792-5522
Fax: 301-792-5557

Page 34
Corrections in lines:
5. New York
6 . Mr. Pace; : (semicolon)
7 . In
8 . would like to

10. September; . (period)
12. . (period)
13. coffee breaks
15. Is it
16. ? (question mark)
17. ? (question mark)
20. Sincerely

Page 35
conversation; plans; confirm; March; rooms; attend; microphone; breaks; questions

Page 37
LETTERS WILL VARY BUT MUST CLOSELY FOLLOW FORMAT PRESENTED IN PART A MODEL LETTER.

UNIT 2B
Page 38
Students circle:
1. B. Mrs. Turner
2. B. January 22
3. B. to confirm information
4. A. Yes
5. B. In Brewster
6. A. M. Dubois

Page 39
1. Thank you for your January 17 letter expressing interest in the Arrowhead Conference Center.
2. This letter will confirm our plans for your meeting.
3a. If you have any questions or need to make any changes, please contact me immediately.
3b. We look forward to seeing you on March 15.

Page 40
1. They; The managers
2. He; The receptionist
3. She; The Vice President
4. He; The planner

1. 1. The mail just arrived.
2. 1. The manager is on the phone.
3. 1. The files are on top of the cabinet.
4. 1. The sales personnel are having a meeting.

Page 41
1. me
2. it
3. her
4. them
5. us

1. My
2. yours
3. Their
4. Our
5. ours

Page 42
Corrections in lines:
2. Ms. Jill Martin (2)
5. Quincy, MA (2)
6. Dear Ms. Martin: (2)
7. you
8. . (period)
10. We; company
15. We
16. If
17. . (period)
19. Sincerely,

21. Katherine
23. F. Jones (3)
24. KP

Page 43
you; your; our; your; your; our; your; you; we; We; you; me; you

Page 45
LETTERS WILL VARY BUT MUST CLOSELY FOLLOW FORMAT PRESENTED IN PART B MODEL LETTER.

UNIT 3A
Page 47
1. supplies
2. purchase order
3. vendor
4. ships
5. fax
6. bills

Page 48
Students circle:
1. A. Yuki Shibata
2. B. In the Purchasing Department
3. A. April 15
4. B. Supplies
5. A. The Purchasing Department

Page 49
1. She ordered copier paper, black pens, red pens, large paper clips.
2. She wants 4 cartons copier paper, 12 dozen black pens, 6 dozen red pens, 5 boxes large paper clips.
3. The Marketing Department will pay.
4. Ms. Shibata will receive the order.
5. The Purchasing Department (Peter Rekowski) will receive the bill.
6. She needs the order ASAP.

Page 50
1. copier paper, black pens, red pens, paper clips
2. Office Supplies
3. Purchasing
4. Marketing
5. $576.13
6. $22.45/doz.
7. $52.38

Page 51
Students circle:
1. A. A purchase orders
2. A. ASAP
3. A. By phone
4. A. A&E Construction

Page 52
1. The purchase order referenced above is enclosed.
2. Please process the order as soon as possible.
3. Thank you for your prompt attention.

1. Don Steele, Chief Executive Officer
2. Katherine Gund, Personnel Director
3. Manual Cabrai, Public Information Officer
4. Bruce Gelb, File Clerk
5. Tina Dresner, Office Manager

Page 53
Students circle:
1. A. An executive desk
2. A. Olson's Office Furniture

3. B. The large one
4. B. HN 31161
5. B. $319.00

Department; Ext.; DATE; SUBJECT; REFERENCE; Order; Desk; Stock; Size; Price; Marketing

Page 55
Corrections in lines:
 4. New Orleans, (comma) (2)
 6. Dear Sir or Madam: (3)
 7. is enclosed. (period) (2)
 8. Please; possible. (period); have (3)
10. (301) 581-2323. (period)
11. attention
12. Sincerely, (comma) (2)

Page 56
MEMOS WILL VARY BUT MUST CLOSELY FOLLOW FORMAT PRESENTED IN PART A MODEL MEMO.

Page 57
LETTERS WILL VARY BUT MUST CLOSELY FOLLOW FORMAT PRESENTED IN PART A MODEL COVER SHEET.

UNIT 3B
Page 58
Students circle:
1. B. Executive Office Supplies
2. B. Yuki Shibata
3. B. Yuki Shibata
4. A. April 22
5. A. April 22
6. A. Yes
7. A. Pens, Black, Item No. P4344
8. A. Yes
9. A. In 3 weeks
10. A. By Monday, April 25

Page 59
1. We received your Purchase Order 02-3450-6 on April 22, 1994.
2. Unfortunately, the item below is not in stock:
3. We will backorder this item and ship it within three (3) weeks.
   OR
   The rest of your order is being processed and will be shipped by Monday, April 25.
4. We appreciate your business and look forward to serving you in the future.

Page 60
Students circle:
1. Sentence; Fragment
2. Fragment; Sentence
3. Fragment; Sentence
4. Sentence; Fragment
5. Sentence; Fragment

Page 61
Corrections in lines:
 5. Mrs. Lawler: (3)
 7. insert "is"
 9. February
10. 1994. (period)
12. January
13. We appreciate your business (3)
14. future. (period)
15. Sincerely yours, (3)

Page 62
Mr.; Drive; Colorado; Dear; Order; December; Desk; order; February; processed; shipped; business; you; yours

Page 63
LETTERS WILL VARY BUT MUST CLOSELY FOLLOW FORMAT PRESENTED IN PART B MODEL LETTER.

UNIT 4A
Page 65
1. page
2. camera
3. first
4. announces
5. wonders

Page 66
Students circle:
1. B. April 5
2. A. Bay State Magazine
3. B. New York
4. B. addressee
5. A. information
6. A. indented

Page 67
Students circle:
1. ? (questions mark)
2. . (period)
3. ? (question mark)
4. . (period)
5. . (period)
6. ? (question mark)
7. . (period)
8. ? (question mark)

Page 68
1. In the April 4, 1993 Boston Daily News I read about your new camera, the XL-Lite.
2. Since I am a photographer with Bay State Magazine, it is important that I know about new cameras.
3a. Would you please send me information on the camera?
3b. I would like to know when the camera will be available and how much it will cost.
4a. Thank you for your attention.
4b. I look forward to your reply.

Page 69
1. in
2. on
3. at
4. on
5. to
6. from
7. in
8. on
9. on
10. at

Page 70
1. stop sending me catalogs.
2. process the order right away?
3. give me the information I need.
4. answer my letter immediately.
5. send me your response right away.

Page 71
Corrections in lines:
 1. August 21, 1994 (2)

2. Inc.
3. Orchard
4. Building; Lane
5. Brewster; NY
6. Sir; Madam: (3)
7. In
8. laboratories. (period); Our
9. equipment. (period)
10. (Could you) please send; laboratories. (period) (2)
11. information? (question mark)
12. Thank; assistance. (period)
13. you. (period)
14. Sincerely yours, (2)
27. Dean

Page 72
August; COMPANY FROM VENDOR LIST; Sir; Madam; In; company; computer; Our; are; looking; products; computers; Would; please; us; educational; include; and; information; Thank; for; attention; forward; Sincerely

Page 73
LETTERS WILL VARY BUT MUST CLOSELY FOLLOW FORMAT PRESENTED IN PART A MODEL LETTER.

UNIT 4B
Page 74
Students circle:
1. A. Click Camera Company
2. B. April 10
3. B. information
4. A. request
5. A. Ms. Jane Wilson (etc.)
6. B. not indented

Page 75
1. Thank you for your letter of April 5, 1993 expressing interest in Click Camera's new camera, the LX-Lite.
2. The camera will be available this December, and the cost will be approximately three hundred and fifty dollars ($350).
3. I have enclosed a brochure on the camera.
4. If you have any questions, please do not hesitate to contact us or your local Click Camera dealer. OR Again, thank you for your inquiry.

Page 76
1. the employees' addresses
2. the vendor's catalog
3. all the companies' policies
4. the secretary's desk
5. the manager's job
6. the vice presidents' offices
7. the company's products
8. the marketing department's meeting
9. the clerks' coffee break
10. the chairman's vacation

Page 77
1. $32; $3; 25
2. 6; 60
3. eleven; 11%; ten; 10%
4. one; 1; one hundred (100)

Page 78
1. I received your catalog but the price list was not enclosed.

2. We will call you or you will receive a letter from us.
3. The package did not arrive but the invoice did.
4. The letter was ready but the mail carrier was late.

Page 79
Corrections in lines:
2. Ms. Ida Roth (3)
3. Jefferson Street (2)
4. Minnesota; delete : (semicolon)
5/6. Dear Ms. Roth: (3)
7. Thank; July 22, (comma)
8. Camera's
9. December
11. If you have
12. dealer. (period)
13. Again; thank; inquiry. (period)
14. yours, (comma)
17. Customer
18. Enclosure

Page 80
Mrs. Carter; you; July __, 1993; interest; available; enclosed; please; not; thank; inquiry

Page 81
LETTERS WILL VARY BUT MUST CLOSELY FOLLOW FORMAT PRESENTED IN PART B MODEL LETTER.

UNIT 5A

Page 83
1. replacement
2. refund
3. credit
4. error
5. overnight mail

Page 84
Students circle:
1. B. no
2. A. yes
3. B. no
4. B. no
5. A. yes
6. A. yes
7. A. yes

Page 85
1. On April 1, I ordered manuals numbers TM-0053-3 and TM-0056-7. On May 7, I received two copies of manual number TM-003553.
2. I am returning — under separate cover — the two training manuals.
3. Please send me the two (2) manuals.
4. Thank you for your assistance.

Page 86
1. Four employees — all in the accounting department — were given raises.
2. The final report — the one with so many changes — was finished on Friday.
3. The entire contents of the package were damaged — stationery, envelopes, and notebooks.
4. All of the supplies were lost during shipping — the books, the paper, the tapes, and the disks.

Page 87
1. Please do not send any brochures.
2. We cannot process the order.
3. We will not ship the supplies without a purchase order.
4. The order was not received last week.
5. The item is not in stock.

Page 88
Corrections in lines:
7. asked for
10. sending back
13. billed for

Page 89
Corrections in lines:
6. Dear Sir or Madam: (4)
7 . This
9 . I am
10. We would; possible. (period)
11. questions. (period); Thank; you
13. Cordially (2)
15. Holly Park (2)

Page 90
TOOLS; Avenue; Houston; TX; November; 94; model; work; like; possible; you; your

Page 91
LETTERS WILL VARY BUT MUST CLOSELY FOLLOW FORMAT PRESENTED IN PART A MODEL LETTER.

UNIT 5B

Page 92
Students circle:
1. A. Mr. Fischer
2. B. Ms. Park
3. A. The wrong manuals were sent.
4. B. He ships them immediately.
5. A. Apologetic
6. B. With the letter
7. A. Paragraph 1
8. B. Paragraph 4

Page 93
1. Thank you for your letter which we received on May 20.
2. We apologize for the error.
3. Two manuals — #TM-0053-3 and #TM-0056-7— will be sent by overnight mail.
4a. Again we regret the error and apologize for any inconvenience.
4b. We look forward to serving you in the future.

Page 94
1. replacement
2. credit
3. refund
4. replacement
5. replacement

1. apology
2. action
3. action
4. apology
5. action

Page 95
1. to type
2. to choose
3. to write

4. to send
5. to find

1. We advised them not to send a refund.
2. Tell him not to ask for full payment.
3. I prefer not to arrive early.
4. He decided not to go.
5. They told us not to miss the meeting.

Page 96
1. to get
2. to apologize
3. to leave
4. to send
5. to fix
6. to know
7. to hear
8. to install

Page 97
Corrections in lines:
8. to (space) your; for
9/10. the (delete); insert "for"; We apologize ... (delete)
11. insert "the"; sent
12. You; them

Page 98
Dr. Brown; you; July; apologize; shipment; overnight; receive; sorry; inconvenience

Page 99
FAXES WILL VARY BUT MUST CLOSELY FOLLOW FORMAT PRESENTED IN PART B MODEL FAX.

UNIT 6A

Page 102
Student circle:
1. B. A payment is overdue.
2. A. Payment
3. B. Foley Construction
4. A. The total amount due
5. A. A reminder
6. B. Ms. Stephens
7. B. On the invoice

1. due
2. full payment
3. balance
4. overdue
5. reminder
6. partial payment

Page 103
Students circle:
1. B. no
2. A. yes
3. B. no
4. A. yes
5. A. yes
6. A. yes
7. A. yes

Page 104
1. Your account balance of $305.56 is now two months overdue.
2. As you know, payment was due on November 1, 1994.
3. If we do not receive payment by January 10, we will have to take appropriate action.
4. We look forward to your prompt response.

Page 105
Students circle:
1. B. The invoice is due tomorrow; send the check today.
2. A. Send a reminder to Mr. Simon, because his account is overdue.
3. B. Please make full payment. An envelope is enclosed.
4. B. The invoice was due yesterday, May 15.
5. B. Your order will be shipped next Friday. You should receive it by July 10.

1. Fragment
2. Run-on
3. Fragment
4. Run-on
5. Run-on

Page 106
Corrections in lines:
7. invoice; was (insert); May; 15. (period)
8. is (delete); Our
9. full (space) payment; 30 (space) days. (period)
10. send (insert); today. (period)
11. look (space) forward; response. (period); We
12. convenience. (period)
13. Sincerely; yours, (delete comma)
14. Accounting Department

Page 107
Corporation; Avenue; Albany; Invoice; Dear; Mr.; Dannon; $456.45; May; full; look; to; Sincerely; yours;

Page 108
LETTERS WILL VARY BUT MUST CLOSELY FOLLOW FORMAT PRESENTED IN PART A MODEL LETTER

PART 6B

Page 109
Students circle:
1. A. Beth Lynch
2. B. Mary Stephens
3. A. January 3
4. A. October 1
5. B. October 30
6. B. Foley Construction

Page 110
1. We received your fax of January 3, 1995.
2. Your invoice 4589-94 dated October 1, 1993 was paid-in-full on October 30, 1993.
3. We are enclosing a copy of the cancelled check which was deposited by your company on November 5.
4. Is you have any questions, please do not hesitate to call.

Page 111
Students circle:
1. ever
2. anything
3. ever
4. fills
5. nor
6. ever

7. anybody
8. anything
9. any
10. nor

Page 113
Accounting; Chicago; received; September; invoice; full; August; August; any; not; call; STUDENT'S INITIALS

Page 115
Atlas Insurance; 45 Southeast Parkway; Los Angeles, California 92187; 916-564-5100; 916-564-5000; DATE WILL VARY; this only/one; received; May; May; full; April; 425; April; any; not; call

Page 117
LETTERS WILL VARY BUT MUST CLOSELY FOLLOW FORMAT PRESENTED IN PART B MODEL LETTER.

FINAL TEST

Page 118
A. Be sure students have applied labels to the following parts of the letter: RETURN ADDRESS, DATE (missing), INSIDE ADDRESS, GREETING OR SALUTATION, BODY, CLOSING (missing), SIGNATURE, TYPED NAME
B. Block
C. Corrections in lines:
1. Ms.
2. Manager
3. Gallery
5. May, 21,; WRONG PLACE; LINE SPACING (4)
6. Houston, Texas (2)
7. Chazam:
8. Thank; May; 1996. (period); I am; DELETE "hear"
9. was; damaged. (period)
10. BLOCK; company
11. would like; I will
12. Smith, not to send
13. books. (period)
14. send; INSERT "Please"
15. arrive (period)
16. RUN-ON SENTENCE
17. DELETE "not"
18. INSERT "I"; forward; future. (period)
21. Shipping

REFERENCE SECTION

Page 123
Exercise 1
1-6. CHECK FOR PROPER FORMAT OF LETTERS.

Page 124
Exercise 2
Return Address; Date; Inside Address; Greeting or Salutation; Body; Closing; Signature; Typed Name

Page 125
Exercise 3
Students cross out:
1. B. Dear Mr. Brown:
2. A. Sincerely yours,
3. C. May 16, 1994
4. A. cc: Dr. Ralph Carson

Exercise 4
1. Milwaukee, Wisconsin
2. Paris, France
3. Seoul, Korea
3. Brisbane, Queensland, Australia
5. Chicago, Illinois
6. Montreal, Quebec, Canada
7. Dallas, Texas
8. Mexico City, DF Mexico

Page 126
Exercise 5
March; April; May; August; September; October; November

Exercise 6
1. July 15, 1992
2. February 9, 1993
3. July 18, 1993
4. October 5, 1992

Exercise 7
1. Do you mean August 12, 1995 or December 8, 1995?
2. Do you mean July 5, 1996 or May 7, 1996?
3. Do you mean November 4, 1997 or April 11, 1997?
4. Do you mean March 10, 1994 or October 3, 1994?
5. Do you mean September 2, 1995 or February 9, 1995?

Page 127
Exercise 8
1. 65 Adams Street
2. 21 Jones Street
3. 145 Rowe Avenue
4. 104 Fifth Avenue

Exercise 9
Students circle:
1. A. Dear Mr. West:
2. B. Dear Mr. Reid:
3. B. Dear Mrs. Tyne:
4. B. Dear Dr. Bier:
5. Dear Mr. Komai:
6. Dear Dr. Locke:
7. Dear Ms. Press:
8. Dear Ms. Burne:

Page 128
Exercise 10
CLOSINGS WILL VARY BUT CHECK FOR FORMAL AND INFORMAL.

Page 130
Exercise 11
Students circle:
1. A. 08887
2. B. 53216
3. A. Wisconsin
4. B. NJ
5. A. WI

Page 131

Exercise 12
Student draw lines between:
1. TO: R. Winston
   FROM: M. Forbet
   DATE: December 15, 1994
   SUB: Health Care
2. TO: G. Bush
   FROM: S. Royce
   DATE: August 8, 1995
   SUB: Travel Insurance
3. TO: M. Crowl
   FROM: S. Marko
   DATE: March 19, 1993
   SUB: Part-time Employees
4. TO: R. Thompson
   FROM: Pete Williams
   DATE: June 17, 1996
   SUBJECT: Employee Benefits

Page 132

Exercise 13
Students circle:
1. B. Liz Ranger
2. A. The staff
3. B. The staff's vacation dates
4. B. Before June 1
5. A. By electronic mail

Page 134

Exercise 14
1. 2
2. 1
3. 4
4. 6
5. 6

Exercise 15
Corrections in lines:
2. January
3. Reservations
4. Ritz Hotel, Paris, France (5)
7. James Grant
8. Manager
9. Pages: This
11. our; morning, (comma); would like
15. my
17. your; hotel. (2)

Page 135

Exercise 16
1. EST
2. 7/2/50
3. DOB
4. NY
5. c/o
6. O/S
7. D/d
8. ASAP
9. VIP

Exercise 17
1. no.
2. Co.
3. St.
4. Dr.
5. STUDENTS INITIALS &
   LAST NAME

Page 136

Exercise 18
1. E. Spain
2. F. Germany
3. G. Japan
4. A. Switzerland
5. C. United Kingdom
6. B. Greece
7. D. Korea
8. H. Austria